Room

FOR

Improvement

Renovation Policies for Older Private Housing

Paul Walentowicz

SHAC
RESEARCH REPORT

SHAC

SHAC opened in 1969 as London's first independent housing aid centre. Its work covers the whole range of housing problems, including homelessness, security of tenure, disrepair and mortgage arrears. Over the past 19 years, SHAC has given advice and help to over 115,000 households.

SHAC's publications and training courses draw on this direct advice-giving experience; it produces a range of advice booklets, publishes research into major housing issues and provides information and training for a wide range of voluntary and statutory organisations.

For further information about SHAC publications, contact the Publications Officer; for details of training courses, contact the Courses and Conferences Organiser (both at SHAC, 189a Brompton Road, London SW5).

SHAC gratefully acknowledges financial assistance from the Department of Environment and the London Borough Grants Unit.

Room For Improvement
Published by SHAC

ISBN 0 948857 22 6

Typesetting, artwork and printing by
RAP Limited
201 Spotland Road
Rochdale OL12 7AF
Tel: (0706) 44981

Trade Distribution — Turnaround 01 609 7836

Acknowledgements

I am grateful to the Nuffield Foundation for making this report possible.

This report could not have been written without the help of many people. I am particularly grateful to the following for their time, trouble and advice.

Hywel Williams of Birmingham, Mike Youkee of the late Greater London Council, Dave Beer of Hammersmith and Fulham, John Perry of Leicester, Mike Martin of Rochdale, Phil Moore of Sheffield and Frank Brakfield of Wandsworth.

Paul Johnson of the Association of District Councils, Matthew Warburton of the Association of London Authorities, Mike Irvine of the Association of Metropolitan Authorities and Sheila Galbraith of the London Boroughs Association.

Ken Taylor of the Abbey National Building Society, Margaret Bunce of the Building Employers Confederation, Mark Boleat of the Building Societies Association, Steve Battersby of the Institution of Environmental Health Officers, Dave McCulloch of the Institute of Housing, Mike McQueen of the Nationwide Anglia Building Society and R.W. Baker of the Royal Institution of Chartered Surveyors.

I also wish to thank my colleagues Karen Smith and Jean Conway who worked together with me on Chapters 6 and 9 respectively. Jean Conway and Geoff Randall also carried out some of the interviews. Many thanks are due to Nadine Nylander who brought the whole report together.

I must add that responsibility for this work, and for any errors of fact or interpretation it contains, is mine alone.

Contents

List of Tables

List of Figures

Abbreviations

AMA	Association of Metropolitan Authorities
BSA	Building Societies Association
DGE	Distribution of Grant Enquiry
DoE	Department of Environment
DSS	Department of Social Security
EHCS	English House Condition Survey
GLHCS	Greater London House Condition Survey
Hansard	All references are to the House of Commons
HCS	Housing and Construction Statistics
HMSO	Her Majesty's Stationery Office
n/a	not available

Recommendations

Central Government

■ The Government must take a firm lead in the formulation and development of an effective policy for older housing. Home improvement should be part of a coherent national housing renewal policy which includes clearance and redevelopment. This requires a clear statement of the aims of improvement, the size and composition of the programme and the balance between improvement and clearance.

■ Improvement is being adversely affected by the cuts taking place in housing expenditure. Unless these are reversed, an effective programme will be virtually impossible. Increased reliance on the private sector will not lead to improved housing conditions in many run-down areas. The occupiers of the poorest quality housing are generally economically weak — many are elderly, low wage or ethnic minority households. A reliance on the market will not help the poor. Ultimately the capacity to renew a worn out stock and reduce inequalities in housing depends on an active programme of public sector-led improvement.

■ National policy should aim to eliminate the core of unsatisfactory private housing revealed by the house condition survey within a decade. This requires an annual programme of 250,000 to 300,000 houses cleared or improved. Financial resources for improvement must return to at least the level of the peak year of 1984. Improved policy instruments will help to focus this expenditure on the worst houses and the poorest households. Extra resources can be found by reforming the regressive tax subsidies to owner occupation.

■ Existing policies are almost entirely remedial and concerned with tackling the backlog of disrepair. New policies must be devised to stimulate regular maintenance and continuing repair.

Local Authorities

■ Variations in local conditions mean that local authorities are best placed to determine local programmes. But central government has a responsibility to set out national priorities and to reflect them in the statutory framework within which local government operates.

■ Local authorities must intensify and speed up their programmes. The Government must provide adequate tools and proper incentives for this to happen.

■ Public sector intervention will range from the distribution of individual improvement grants, to more intensive area approaches, to acquisition by local authorities and housing associations. The most appropriate course of action is best decided at the local level.

■ Local programmes need to be better integrated with wider housing programmes, other inner city initiatives and planning policies.

Home Improvement Grants

■ Improvement by individual owners with the help of a grant is likely to remain the most frequent method adopted to achieve high standard improvement. SHAC welcomes the Government's endorsement of a unitary grant to replace the existing four separate grants and the removal of some eligibility restrictions. The concept of mandatory grant to bring a property up to the fitness standard is also to be welcomed but the plan to base grant entitlement on a means-test related to housing benefit is a retrograde step.

■ All households should be eligible for a grant irrespective of their income falling one side or another of an arbitrary threshold. Grant rates should reflect the degree of priority accorded to the necessary work and the needs of the applicant. The minimum rate of mandatory grant should be 75 per cent with a maximum of 100 per cent based on the actual cost of the work. Discretionary grants should be available at a minimum rate of 50 per cent up to a maximum of 90 per cent. Households in receipt of a social security benefit should receive the maximum rate. Grants in improvement areas should be mandatory.

Area Improvement

■ There remains a strong case for an intensive approach to improvement in areas where unsatisfactory housing, inadequate facilities and a poor environment are concentrated. Area policies have important advantages in stimulating confidence and self-help. Area improvement can be made to work but too few areas have been declared. More declarations are needed. Greater incentives and subsidies are required.

■ SHAC welcomes the proposal to simplify the procedures by replacing GIAs and HAAs with a single type of improvement area — a Housing Renewal Area. But areas need additional financial resources to succeed. An effective package must include extra incentives for households and local authorities — a priority rate of grant, no-cost envelope schemes, increased subsidy for environmental improvements and strengthened local authority powers.

Home Improvement Agencies

■ Agencies can encourage work which might not have taken place otherwise, reduce many of its pitfalls and make any expenditure more effective. More agencies are needed. Most useful are those which provide general advice and offer a range of choices and options. The Government's support for agencies is recognised. It must make a commitment to fund more agencies either directly itself or via voluntary organisations or local authorities. Private sector agencies may be able to play a part in areas with less serious problems. Agencies may have an important future role in encouraging regular maintenance and repair and in promoting 'after-care'in former statutory areas.

Improvement Incentives

■ More effective incentives to encourage repair and improvement are a priority. Grants and agencies cannot reach everyone. The rate of VAT on repairs and improvements should be reduced. New schemes to encourage saving for future expenditure should be examined. There is considerable potential for the development and promotion of attractive loan packages, including maturity loans. Equity release schemes which boost the incomes of elderly households offer hope for the future. More generous social security help should be available to the poorest households. The existing tax subsidies and incentives to owner occupiers do not encourage maintenance or repair. They should be reduced to provide more resources for new measures to stimulate renovation. A comprehensive housing allowance scheme, to replace mortgage tax relief and housing benefit, would lower the burden of occupancy costs and allow people to spend more on renovation.

■ Ignorance about the importance of property maintenance and a lack of confidence in the building industry also inhibit adequate maintenance and repair. The Government should take the lead and mount a long-term publicity campaign to increase public awareness and knowledge. Warranty or guarantee schemes offered by the building industry can help to overcome fears about problems with builders. The standard of improvement work needs to be raised.

Housing Standards

■ The present fitness standard is out of date and omits some important health and safety items. The government's proposed new standard is too low. A new minimum housing standard should apply to all types of housing.

It should include all the requirements of the existing fitness standard, all the standard amenities plus electrical wiring, means of access and escape in case of fire, artificial lighting and space heating. Houses below this standard should be improved or removed from the stock. Local authorities should be under a duty to take action against an unfit house within a specified period of time.

Ethnic Minority Home Owners

■ Asian and black owners, in general, occupy older properties which provide fewer amenities and are in poorer condition than those of white owners. On average, they have lower incomes than white owners. In so far as a low income deters people from undertaking renovation work, the proposals for a better targeted grant scheme should concentrate help. The public and private sectors should provide specific services to assist ethnic minority owners who have repair or improvement problems and should aim to eliminate discrimination in service provision and delivery. Specific recommendations include: ethnic monitoring of grant and mortgage approvals; house condition surveys should seek information on race and house condition; local authorities and agency services (where appropriate) should focus publicity about grants, and offer practical assistance, to ethnic minority owners. Local authorities should also examine their grant procedures and requirements to see if any place ethnic minority owners at a disadvantage.

Private Rented Housing

■ Improvement and enforcement activity in the rented sector is too low. Few grants are made to private landlords. Market rents are not the solution. A reformed system which links grants to house condition and rental income should encourage increased activity. Compulsory powers to deal with poor quality rented housing should be strengthened and the cumbersome procedures streamlined. Powers to deal with unsafe, sub-standard or badly managed HMOs are in particular need of overhaul. Tenants should have access to effective remedies.

CHAPTER 1

Introduction

The Problem

The deteriorating state of the housing stock in Britain is now widely regarded as one of the most major current housing problems. It was, for instance, one of the four key concerns addressed by the recent *'Inquiry into British Housing'* chaired by the Duke of Edinburgh. One in four — about 3.5 million houses — of England's private sector housing is officially classified as unsatisfactory. It is deteriorating faster than it is being repaired or replaced. The crisis of disrepair is striking all tenures, although conditions in the private rented sector remain the poorest. The scale of public attention and financial resources devoted to improving housing conditions is not sufficient to meet this crisis.

This report highlights the deterioration of the older private sector stock. Its aim is to contribute to the debate on house renovation by examining current practice, surveying its strengths and limitations, and recommending changes in future policies and practice to halt and reverse housing decay.

Background

For over a century British governments have been concerned with the condition of privately owned housing. The problem has been tackled by removing the worst housing and replacing it with new homes built to a higher standard. Slum clearance and redevelopment reached its zenith in the late 1960s. The emphasis in housing policy shifted in the 1970s to the improvement, rather than the replacement, of older houses. The impact of these programmes has been massive. Two million houses have been demolished since the 1930s. Over three million have been improved with government help since the end of the last war. This huge state sponsored enterprise has resulted in great changes to the physical and social fabric of urban areas.

Yet, despite all this activity, unsatisfactory housing conditions remain. As the slums have been cleared or improved, new problems have emerged. While substantial progress has been made in providing existing housing with the basic amenities, disrepair and decay has gradually been recognised as a growing issue. The growth of home ownership has increased the number of owners, many of them elderly or from an ethnic minority, who are unable to afford to look after their homes. An emerging generation of 'marginal' owner occupiers, represents a dilemma for a housing policy aimed at encouraging the tenure's growth. The housing market and the system of housing finance favour house purchase but not house repair or maintenance.

The shift of policy from comprehensive redevelopment to improvement has been accompanied by an overall reduction in activity. The downward trend has fluctuated — with brief booms in subsidised improvements in the early 1970s and 1980s. Central government support has contracted from an annual programme of 240,000 houses cleared or improved in the early 1970s to 120,000 today (**Figure One**). Housing has borne the brunt of the public expenditure cutbacks of recent years.

Figure I   Grant Aided Renovations and Slum Clearance, 1971-1987, England

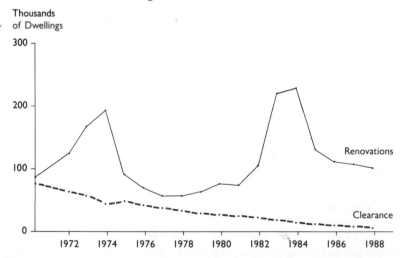

The scale of activity has not kept pace with the rate of physical deterioration. As a result the backlog of disrepair is growing, and some houses are declining into unfitness. These processes have been documented by successive surveys of the national housing stock. It is widely accepted, largely for economic reasons, that there cannot be a return to the large scale clearance and redevelopment programmes of earlier years. Housebuilding by the private sector is generally meeting the needs of new households and is not replacing old worn-out housing. Much of the existing stock is therefore ageing rapidly. In 1971 about 1.75 million private sector homes in Britain were over 100 years old. By 1991 the number will have doubled. But this stock will have to go on being used and lived in.

The magnitude of the problem, and the prospect that it may worsen considerably in the very near future, dictates the need for a thorough review of existing improvement policies.

The Government's Plans

The Government is planning a sweeping reform of improvement policies. Its plans include major changes to the improvement grant system. These reforms, which require new legislation, will come into effect early in 1990. Many critics have suggested that they signal the end of positive intervention by the public sector and of the tradition of state concern for social inequality in housing. The Government's plans were initially outlined in a Green Paper published in May 1985. Since then they have been both modified and amplified but have as yet received little critical assessment or evaluation. This report looks at the Government's plans in some detail.[1]

A Fresh Look at Improvement Policy

Private sector housing is increasingly beset by decay and disrepair. Insufficient resources are being channelled towards house improvement. Current policies do not match the problem. The impact of the Government's proposals for the future needs to be considered. If the housing stock is allowed to deteriorate further, many more houses will decay to the stage where demolition and rehousing are the only options. Given the age of the stock, this would entail a risk of a great surge in public spending on clearance and redevelopment later this century. A policy of benign neglect now will cost much more in the future. The issue then is not whether, but how, a vigorous programme is constructed.

SHAC has been concerned about the condition of the housing stock for many years, and has considerable experience with repair and improvement policy through its training, advice and research activities. In 1981, SHAC published a report '*Good Housekeeping: An Examination of Housing Repair and Improvement Policy*', which analysed the problem of sub-standard housing and current policies for tackling it, as well as putting forward recommendations for reform. Most remain valid today. Its main recommendations are given in **Appendix One**. This report builds on that earlier work.

The time is ripe for a fresh look at improvement policies. The objective must be a policy framework which encourages regular maintenance of the housing stock and which enables defective houses to be brought up to standard. Primary responsibility for looking after private housing must rest with its owners. The government has, however, a responsibility for creating conditions which encourage personal responsibility and initiative, increase private investment and make it more effective. Improvement must be a partnership between public and private sectors. Problems of low investment in maintenance and repair are partly attributable to a lack of household resources. Occupiers of the poorest quality housing are generally economically weak — among them many elderly households, low wage earners or people from an ethnic minority. Most cannot afford to put their homes into a satisfactory condition. A reliance on the private sector will do little for the urban poor. The Government has done much to enable many to become home owners: more must be done to enable them to remain so. Ultimately, the capacity to renew a worn out stock and reduce inequality in housing is dependent on a high enough level of public spending.

Local authorities are best placed to determine local renewal programmes. But central government has a responsibility to set out national priorities and to reflect them in the statutory framework within which local authorities operate. The most appropriate balance between clearance and improvement, and priorities between individual properties which are to be improved, are largely matters for local judgement. For some houses which are unfit, the only real choice is demolition. The pendulum has probably swung too far against clearance.

Central government intervenes directly itself in the housing market, most notably by encouraging home ownership in the form of tax relief on mortgage interest payments. This intervention does nothing to encourage maintenance or repair. In fact, it may actively discourage it. It is a highly inefficient source of support because it gives most help to those who need it least. It operates to the disadvantage of low income households. Rationalisation of housing finance is long overdue, and could well provide extra resources for an invigorated improvement programme.

The scale of the problem of house condition means there is an urgent need for a national programme to eliminate the core of unsatisfactory housing within a decade. Achievement of this aim would require an annual programme of around 250,000 — 300,000 private sector houses cleared or improved and a return to the expenditure levels of the years 1982-84. Improved policy instruments should help to focus this expenditure on the worst houses and poorest households. There is no shortage of new ideas. Many involve a recasting of existing policies; others build on innovations of recent years. This report draws on these ideas. Prevention is better than cure and is usually cheaper. Regular maintenance carried out throughout the life of a house delays the problem of disrepair. More indirect measures to stimulate self-help and investment by private households will go a long way to stemming the decay of the housing stock.

Its Limitations

This report is concerned solely with the structure and scope of the official response to the specific issue of poor housing conditions in the private sector. But this response has inherent limitations because it is primarily concerned with the symptoms of urban decline — bad housing, environmental decay — and not with its causes.

Central government's advice to local authorities suggests that improvement policies should concentrate on:

'...removing the underlying causes of the housing stress in the area...'[2]

The 'underlying causes' of housing stress and the deterioration of the housing stock in urban areas are economic, not physical. The prime cause is the decline of the urban economy. Poor housing is then but one symbol of economic forces which lead to an unequal distribution of income and wealth. Housing policy cannot remove the 'underlying causes' of housing decay. But it can effectively tackle some of its symptoms. Such a policy is limited to improving physical housing conditions and cannot be expected to provide a solution to economic inequality. It is not unreasonable in this context to discuss policies designed to increase the rate of improvement and to make substantial progress in dealing with housing obsolescence.

Research Methods

Research for this report consisted of three main elements:

- Analysis of published material on the problem of sub-standard housing and on the operation of the renovation grant system and other policy instruments designed to encourage improvement activity. This included reference to statistical returns, official surveys and reports as well as secondary material.
- Contact, discussions and data obtained from central and local government. A sample of local authorities were interviewed in depth to examine their perceptions of current practice, its merits and defects, and to elicit their views on possible alternative approaches.
- Interviews with private sector institutions, including builders' organisations and building societies, and local authority associations and professional organisations were also conducted. The aim was to ascertain their views on the renewal of private housing and the policies to encourage it, including

the renovation grant system, and the potential for public-private sector co-operation.

Structure of the Report

The report:

- discusses the deterioration of and the prospects for the private sector housing stock
- looks at existing practice and assesses the Government's proposed reforms
- puts forward recommendations for future home improvement policies

The structure of the report is as follows:

Chapter 2 looks at the extent of unsatisfactory house conditions in the private sector. It highlights the characteristics of those households who occupy the worst housing. It shows that very few have the resources to improve their homes. It goes on to discuss the link between a low level of improvement activity and inefficiencies in the housing market.

Chapter 3 assesses the prospects for the housing stock and improvement within the wider housing and expenditure policies and priorities of the Government.

The following chapters examine in detail the range of current policies to encourage home improvement, assess (where relevant) the Government's proposals, and suggest practical reforms.

Chapter 4 deals with home improvement grants to private owners;

Chapter 5 with local authority powers to deal with concentrations of houses in poor condition;

Chapter 6 with services which advise and help individual owners with repair or improvement problems;

Chapter 7 with a range of incentives, provided by both the public and private sectors, to encourage improvement;

Chapter 8 with housing standards.

The Government has failed to consider the special interests, needs and problems of ethnic minority home owners and has virtually ignored the acute problems found in the private rented sector. *Chapters 9* and *10* examine these issues respectively.

Summary

Disrepair in the private sector is a serious problem. It requires an equally serious response. Earlier intervention partially broke the link between income and housing conditions. The Government appears committed to minimising the role of the public sector in maintaining good housing standards. This cannot be sustained. It fails to recognise that as our heritage of Victorian and Edwardian housing slips into its second century there are real limits to how far it can withdraw from the fray. Alone among political institutions it has a longevity to match that of houses which have stood for a century and which will have to go on standing for perhaps a century more. This report urges a more forthright and determined response from the Government.

References

1. DoE/Welsh Office, *Home Improvement — A New Approach* Cmnd. 9513, HMSO, 1985 (Green Paper, 1985)
    DoE/Welsh Office, *Housing: The Goverment's Proposals* Cmnd. 214, HMSO, 1987 (White Paper, 1987)
2. DoE, Circular 14/75, para. 35

CHAPTER **2**

The Drift into Disrepair

The first part of this chapter looks at the condition of the private sector housing stock in England as shown by the 1981 and preceding house condition surveys. For London alone more recent information is available from the 1985 regional survey. The second looks at the characteristics and resources of the occupiers of the worst housing. The third outlines some of the links between home improvement activity and the housing market.[1]

Condition of the Stock

There were 12.5 million private sector homes in England in 1981. Much of this stock is elderly: nearly 40 per cent was built before 1919.[2]

No less than 900,000 (7 per cent) were unfit, 600,000 (5 per cent) still lacked basic amenities and over 3 million (25 per cent) needed repairs costing more than £2,500.[3] Allowing for the overlap between these categories the total number of unsatisfactory private sector houses is 3.5 million or 28 per cent of the stock.[4]*

---

*An *unfit* house is one deemed so far defective in one or more of the following matters as not to be reasonably suitable for occupation: repair, stability, freedom from damp, internal arrangement, natural lighting, ventilation, water supply, drainage and sanitary conveniences, facilities for the preparation and cooking of food and the disposal of waste water. The fitness standard is discussed in more detail in *Chapter 8*.

The five *basic* or *standard* amenities are: a bath or shower, a wash basin, a kitchen sink, a hot and cold water supply serving them and the exclusive use of a wc inside the dwelling.

Unsatisfactory houses are those which were unfit, lacked basic amenities or needed repairs costing over £2,500 at 1981 prices.´

Over recent years there has been a significant reduction in the number of private sector homes lacking amenities. Reliable evidence of quantitative change in unfitness is more difficult to establish. This is because retrospective adjustments were made, for technical reasons, to the results of earlier surveys by the DoE. The revised figures for 1976 suggest that the extent of housing unfitness was originally underestimated by over 50 per cent. Consequently the trend in unfitness appears more favourable than it would otherwise have done. Even so, the number of unfit dwellings only declined moderately after 1976.

In one vital area the position is getting worse: the number of private sector homes needing major repairs (i.e. those costing over £7,000) increased by 17 per cent since the stock was last surveyed in 1976. No comparison is possible at lower levels of repair costs owing to the unreliability of the data.[5]

Table I   Change in Private Sector House Conditions, England (thousands of dwellings)

	1971	1976	1981
Unfit	985 (924)[2]	902 (597)[2]	853
Lacking at least one basic amenity	2,112	1,054	622
Needing repairs costing over £2,500[1]	n/a	n/a	3,064
Needing repairs costing over £7,000[1]	777	754	882

Notes: (1) 1981 prices.
      (2) Figures in brackets are original results
Source: EHCS, 1982, tables E,H, and L

Evidence of housing decay from the 1981 national survey can be supplemented by the results of the 1985 London survey. It found that of the 1.6 million private sector homes in London, 400,000 (25 per cent) were in unsatisfactory condition.[6] **Table 2** shows some of the changes in London's housing conditions since the equivalent 1979 survey.*

Progress has been made in tackling unfitness and lack of amenities but there has been no net improvement in the incidence of disrepair. Although the picture in London is not representative of the country as a whole, particularly since it is drawn over a different period of time, these results lend support to the general trends found by the earlier national survey. Disrepair is a serious problem, while unfitness and lack of basic amenities appear to be declining in importance.

Unsatisfactory houses in London are those which were unfit, lacked basic amenities or needed repairs costing over £5,300 at 1985 prices.

Table 2   Change in Private Sector House Conditions, Greater London (thousands of dwellings)

	1979	1985
Unfit	158	94
Lacking at least one basic amenity	139	55
Needing repairs costing over £5,300[1]	362	364
Needing repairs costing over £9,000[1]	192	194

Note: (1) 1985 prices
Source: GLHCS, 1987, tables 26, 29 and 37

Since the end of the war much obsolete housing has either been demolished and replaced or improved up to a modern standard. Poor housing is now chiefly characterised by disrepair, and less by intrinsic factors such as internal arrangement, poor natural lighting or the absence of amenities. Such problems are finite in number, and can only be reduced, whereas disrepair is an active, if gradual, process and one which can move in either direction. Whatever the precise trends since the early 1970s, there is no room for complacency when even the Government's own research shows that there were 3.5 million unsatisfactory private sector houses in England in 1981. The latest estimate of the cost of repairing all of these is £30 billion.[7] For London alone, the repair bill for the private sector was estimated to be £6.6 billion in 1985.[8] The national survey report rightly concluded that 'The scope for further impact on the worst housing hinges ... on the extent to which disrepair is tackled'.[9]

Age and Condition

Poor housing is heavily concentrated in the pre-1919 stock, particularly in terraced property with low rateable values. In England only one in every twenty private sector homes needing expensive repairs was built after 1919.

Table 3   Unsatisfactory Private Sector Houses by Age, 1981, England (% of dwellings)

	Pre-1919	Post-1919
Unfit	91%	9%
Needing repairs costing over £2,500[1]	78%	22%
Needing repairs costing over £7,000[1]	95%	5%

Note: (1) 1981 prices
Source: EHCS, 1982, tables 13 and 21

But poor conditions in the inter-war stock is an emerging problem. The percentage of unfit private sector homes among those built in the inter-war period increased from about 2 per cent in 1971 to 8 per cent in 1981 and the proportion of those with high repair costs almost doubled over the decade.[10] This probably reflects the concentration of grant-aided improvement activity in the pre-1919 stock as well as the fact that the inter-war stock is itself now of some considerable vintage.

Location and Condition

A greater proportion of homes in poor condition are found in the conurbations and rural areas than in provincial towns.[11] Nearly a half of unfit houses and over a third of those in serious disrepair are located in potential statutory improvement areas. Area improvement is discussed in *Chapter 5.*[12]

Tenure and Condition

When the different tenures are compared private rented homes remain in substantially worse, and local authority homes in slightly better, condition than those in owner occupation. The private rented sector is looked at in some detail in *Chapter 10.* There have been significant shifts in the last decade in the absolute number of poor dwellings in each tenure. In 1971 the private rented sector contained most unfit homes, most lacking amenities and most in serious disrepair. But by 1981 the largest number of homes in all these categories was found in the owner occupied sector. This trend is a result of the substantial growth in recent years of the owner occupied sector and the reduction in size of the private rented sector.[13]

Table 4   Unsatisfactory Owner Occupied Houses, England (thousands of dwellings and as a % of the total unsatisfactory stock)

	1971	%	1981	%
Unfit	356	29	483	43
Lacking at least one basic amenity	945	34	340	37
Needing repairs costing over £2,500[(1)]	n/a	n/a	2,189	56
Needing repairs costing over £7,000[(1)]	314	36	539	51

Notes: (1) 1981 prices.
Source: EHCS, 1982, tables E,H, L and 21

A similar development has occurred in London. Almost a half of London's unsatisfactory housing is owner occupied, compared with 39 per cent in 1979.[14]

Table 5   Unsatisfactory Owner Occupied Houses, Greater London (thousands of dwellings and as a % of the total unsatisfactory stock)

	1979	%	1985	%
Unfit	68	28	55	39
Lacking at least one basic amenity	45	19	22	21
Needing repairs costing over £5,300[1]	208	44	251	50
Needing repairs costing over £9,000[1]	96	37	129	53

Notes: (1) 1985 prices.
Source: GLHCS, 1987, tables 26, 29 and 37

The increase in unfitness (up by 36 per cent) and disrepair (up by 72 per cent) in the owner occupied sector across the country has important implications for future renewal policies particularly if, as seems likely, it is not a phenomenon confined to the 1970s and early 1980s.[15] The shift in the tenurial incidence of poor housing is a reflection of the growth of home ownership in Britain; a development especially marked in the older housing stock. In 1970 17 per cent of building society mortgages were on a property built before 1919 but by 1988 this proportion had grown to 26 per cent.[16] There is, as we have already seen, a close relation between the age and the condition of a property. Almost all of the owner occupied housing which is in serious disrepair was built before 1919.[17] By 1981 over 2 million owner occupied homes needed repairs costing over £2,500 — one fifth of the total owner occupied stock.[18] The issue facing the country is whether present, and future, owners have either the resources or the incentive to keep their increasingly elderly homes in good repair.

Households in the Poorest Housing

Results from the 1981 *English House Condition Survey* (EHCS) social survey allow some conclusions to be drawn about the characteristics of households living in the poorest conditions in England.[19]

Households living in unfit homes are more likely to be elderly, retired, unemployed, poor or long-standing residents. Households living in the worst unfit housing stand in even greater contrast to those in satisfactory dwellings. Over the period 1976 to 1981 the only two major trends in the 'unfit' population were proportional increases in owner occupiers, long-term residents and households with nobody in paid employment. In 1976, for example, 30 per cent of unfit housing was occupied by households with no one in work, but by 1981 this had risen to 47 per cent.[20]

The absence of amenities, whether or not combined with unfitness or disrepair, is more a feature associated with the elderly. Although 29 per cent of all households are headed by somebody of retirement age, this is so for 55 per cent of people lacking one or more basic amenities and 61 per cent lacking a bath.[21]

Table 6 shows that households living in the poorest stock have lower average incomes than those in satisfactory homes. Moreover the least well off live in homes needing the highest average expenditure to remedy the defects, and are more likely to be people with limited economic opportunities such as the elderly or the unemployed.

Table 6   Household Characteristics and House Condition, 1981, England (% of households)

	Satisfactory Dwellings	Unfit Dwellings	Unfit and in Serious Disrepair
Age of household head			
Retirement age	27	43	47
(aged 75-98 years)	9	19	23
Economic inactivity			
Household head retired	22	33	38
Zero household members in work	29	47	53
Income and savings			
Median annual income	£5570	£2600	£2200
Annual income under £2200	27	n/a	62
Median savings	£223	n/a	£195
No savings	27	35	36
Length of residence			
Resident for over 20 years	25	48	59

Source: EHCS, 1983, tables A,5,6,7,9,10 and 11.

Resources and Renovation Costs

The survey examined in some detail the ability of households to put their homes into good order by comparing the cost of carrying out the necessary work with household resources.

In the absence of financial help very few households in the poorer stock could fund the remedial work from their current savings. Less than 10 per cent of those in homes found to be unfit or in serious disrepair could do so, compared with over one half of those in the satisfactory stock. The great majority would have to find a sum of at least three times their current savings.[22] The survey also confirmed that many households living in poor conditions would have to spend a substantial proportion of their income if they had to finance the cost of any work by loan repayments. **Table 7** looks more closely at the financial circumstances of owner occupiers.

Table 7   **Full Cost of Remedial Work as a Proportion of Annual Income (Owner Occupiers only), 1981, England (% of households)**

	Satisfactory Dwellings	Unfit Dwellings	Unfit and in Serious Disrepair
0%-100%	97	26	6
101%-300%	3	34	30
301% or more	0	40	64

Note: Gross household income
Source: EHCS, 1983, tables I and 28.

Three-quarters of the owner occupiers of unfit, and almost all living in the very worst housing would need to spend more than their annual gross incomes to bring their homes up to standard. Two-thirds of those living in the very worst stock would need to spend more than three times their income. The majority of such households have no member in paid employment usually because they are over retirement age.[23] They would find it almost impossible to raise or pay for a loan from a bank or building society. Few lenders are prepared to advance more than 2½ to 3 times someone's income. Even if they could secure a loan, most would find the repayments an impossible burden.[24] It follows that the great majority are unable to pay for repairs or essential improvements to their homes from income, or to accumulate sufficient savings.

Expenditure on Home Improvements

Most of the improvement, repair and maintenance work undertaken by private owners takes place without grant aid or other specific government incentives (except for tax relief on the interest of improvement loans which was removed in the 1988 budget). The 1981 EHCS found that in the five years preceding the survey about 60 per cent of owner occupied homes had had some major work done to them.[25] The total value of all types of work in any year is difficult to quantify with certainty but is estimated to be about £10 billion a year.[26] Of this less than £200 million came from improvement grants. Much of this expenditure is, however, on non-essential works of improvement such as the installation of central heating or the replacement of bathroom or kitchen fitments rather than works which could be unequivocally labelled remedial. Although such works undoubtedly enhance the comfort, convenience and lifestyle of the household they do not relate to the physical fabric of the building.[27]

But about one-fifth of homes had no major or minor works on them at all in 1981 and the overall average expenditure per dwelling was dominated by the minority for which large expenditures were recorded.[28] The most common amount spent on home improvements and remedial works in 1981 by the owner occupiers of pre-1919 properties was £120.[29] Moreover there appeared to be little variation of expenditure with the age of the dwelling indicating that the more modern housing was receiving greater attention in relation to its need.[30]

A guide to trends in spending on home improvements can be obtained from the *Family Expenditure Survey* which shows actual weekly expenditure on repairs, maintenance and decoration by households but excludes expenditure on alterations and work financed by loans. It reveals wide variations in real spending levels between different parts of the country over recent years.

Average expenditure by home owners in the economically depressed regions, which also have high proportions of older housing, has not even kept pace with inflation. In the prosperous South East, however, spending has more than kept pace with rising costs (**Table 8**).

Low Income Home Ownership

Another development, which may lead to problems in the future, is the fact that owner occupation has gradually been extending down the income scale to include people who are, at best, only just able to afford the costs of ownership. The rise in the proportion of homes in owner occupation over recent years (up by 12 per cent since 1973) is paralleled by the increased proportion of semi and unskilled manual workers who now own their homes. In 1973, for example, 9 per cent of owner occupiers with a mortgage were semi-skilled manual workers, by 1985 the proportion had increased to 34 per cent.[31] Low

Table 8   Expenditure⁽¹⁾ by Owner Occupiers on Repair, Maintenance and Decorations by Region

	North		North West		West Midlands		Greater London		Rest of South East		Repair and Maintenance Cost Indices[2]	
	£pw	index	£pw	index	£pw	index	£pw	index	£pw	index	Materials	Average Earnings
1979-80	4.54	100	4.02	100	3.47	100	3.37	100	4.39	100	100	100
1980-81	3.78	83	3.65	91	3.76	108	4.54	135	4.56	104	108	113
1981-82	3.62	80	3.95	98	4.20	121	4.95	147	4.82	110	117	123
1982-83	3.25	72	4.59	114	4.85	140	5.20	154	5.20	118	125	133
1983-84	3.40	75	5.07	126	4.40	127	7.35	218	6.23	142	134	141
1984-85	3.14	69	5.60	139	3.92	113	7.93	235	7.57	172	142	152
1985-86	4.75	105	5.47	136	4.26	123	7.60	226	11.40	260	146	164

Note: (1) Average of outright and purchasing owners
　　　(2) Calendar year

Source: Family Expenditure Survey, various years
　　　　HCS, 1976-1986, 1987

income households often purchase older houses which are already in poor condition simply because that is all they can afford. Once bought they have fewer resources to pay for repairs or maintenance. Such households often need to borrow up to the limit to finance their entry into owner occupation. The ratio of the average mortgage advance to the average income of first-time buyers rose from 1.67 in 1980 to over 2 in 1987. The average mortgage advance rose from 73.8 per cent to around 85 per cent of the average house price over the same period.[32] Some households have to borrow from less orthodox sources, such as fringe banks, who charge higher than average interest rates and many take out additional loans to buy furniture or other essentials.[33] The incidence of mortgage arrears is proof that more and more owners are facing insuperable financial problems. The number of building society borrowers over six months in arrears has risen rapidly since 1979 to over 60,000 by the end of 1987. Building societies also took a record number of properties (22,630) into possession in 1987.[34] Mortgage arrears is now a significant cause of homelessness. In 1987 about one in every ten families was accepted as homeless by a local authority because of mortgage arrears compared with less than one in every twenty in 1979.[35]

A recent study of five inner city areas in Birmingham and Liverpool found that a large proportion of the residents who were owner occupiers had low incomes and had bought a home only because of a lack of other options. Many had bought in haste without paying proper attention to the condition of the property. A third had looked at only the house they purchased and many did not have the benefit of professional advice about its state of repair. In these areas the proportion of building society loans was much lower than the national average. It was also found that property had lost value relative to the region in which it was situated. In one area of Birmingham, where stagnation of house prices was worst, buyers — many of whom were Asian — would have been better-off if they had rented a home and invested their savings. However because their chance of finding a suitable property to rent was slight, they had little alternative but to buy no matter how bad a bargain it was.

Disrepair was a serious problem. Over a half of the longer established owners had postponed doing major repairs, usually because they could not pay for them. A few had received an improvement grant but this only covered between a third and a half of total expenditure. The estimated cost of the work needed on these houses was, on average, greater than the price paid to buy them. Faced with the evidence of a widening gap between the circumstances of these and similar inner city owner occupiers and the tenure as a whole, the study argued that a substantial level of financial and other support was essential. This could only come from the public sector.[36]

Housing Market Inefficiency

It would be inaccurate to suggest that the only explanation for inadequate expenditure on repairs and maintenance is that many owners are too poor. Certainly the low incomes of some is the major factor. But the formation of areas of poor housing often depends on additional factors which suggest that the housing market operates inefficiently as well as inequitably. The market undoubtedly undervalues improvement activity. Potential improvers may be discouraged by the fact that the post-improvement increase in the value of a property is often less than the cost of the improvements — a phenomenon known as the 'valuation gap' **(Figure 2).** The worse the condition of a property, the bigger the valuation gap is likely to be. The disincentive effect is increased if an unimproved property can be sold at a profit gained through house price inflation. The difference between the cost of any work to a house and its subsequent value not only discourages improvement but means that it is frequently cheaper to buy a better house elsewhere than carry out major repairs.

Figure 2   The Valuation Gap

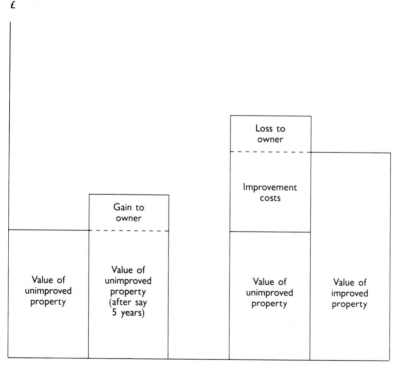

The valuation gap is linked to what economists call 'neighbourhood externalities', which have also been thought to lead to a lack of maintenance and repair and thus to a gradual deterioration of the properties within an area. The effect is likely to be pronounced on the borders of areas of bad housing where the decision whether to look after a property, or to let it decline in a similar way as the neighbouring houses, is often faced. The mechanism, in brief, works as follows: because the value of a property depends not only upon its intrinsic qualities but also on those of other properties in the vicinity, an owner may be deterred from improving it because of the fear that any benefits will be jeopardised by the external costs imposed on her or his property by unimproved adjoining ones. Because each owner gains if all the others spend money on renovating their homes whilst not doing so her or himself, nobody does so, and therefore everyone loses. However if they all renovated, they would all be better off. This uncertainty about the intentions of one's neighbours is a vivid illustration of the classic 'prisoner's dilemma.'[37]

Summary

House conditions in the private sector are deteriorating. The owner occupied sector now accounts for the largest proportion of bad housing in England. The occupiers of the worst houses are more likely to be elderly, retired, unemployed or poor. Few can afford to finance the necessary remedial work from their income or savings and most have little chance of ever being able to do so. Spending on repair and maintenance by many private owners shows no sign of increasing in real terms. The outlook is made bleaker by the growth of 'marginal' owner occupation. Market imperfections may also contribute to the perceived inadequacy of renovation activity by private owners. The increased incidence of poor housing conditions is the most visible sign of economic recession, urban decay and deprivation. The result is the emergence of an expanding core of bad private housing, accommodating increasing concentrations of low income occupiers. This national scandal represents the failure of previous housing renewal policies and the failure to adapt them to meet new situations.

References

1. DoE, English House Condition Survey 1981, HMSO Part 1 Report of the Physical Condition Survey, 1982 (EHCS, 1982)
    Part 2 Report of the Interview and Local Authority Survey, 1983 (EHCS, 1983)
    AMA, Greater London House Condition Survey 1985, AMA, 1987 (GLHCS, 1987)
2. Green Paper, 1985, para. 6
3. EHCS, 1982, tables 5, 13 and 21
4. Green Paper, 1985, para.5
5. EHCS, 1982, para.23 and Appendix II
6. GLHCS, 1987, para. 2 and table 3
7. AMA, *Less Ruin: More Renewal*, 1986, para.2, p.3
8. GLHCS, 1987, figure 23
9. EHCS, 1983, para. 2.21
10. EHCS, 1982, tables 13, 21 and 41
11. EHCS, 1982, table 19
12. EHCS, 1982, tables 15 and 25

13. EHCS, 1982, tables E, H and L
14. GLHCS, 1987, p.9 and Greater London Council, 1979 GLHCS, 1981, tables 3.1 and 5.2
15. EHCS, 1982, tables H and L
16. *BSA Bulletin* No.48, October 1986, p.9 and No.55, July 1988, table 14
17. EHCS, 1982, table 21
18. ibid
19. EHCS, 1983, op cit
20. EHCS, 1983, table C
21. EHCS, 1983, table B
22. EHCS, 1983, table H
23. EHCS, 1983, table J
24. EHCS, 1983, table K
25. EHCS, 1983, table 39
26. DoE, Circular 16/88, para. 10
27. EHCS, 1983, para. 6.7
28. EHCS, 1983, para. 6.3
29. EHCS, 1983, table O
30. EHCS, 1983, para. 6.3 and figure 36
31. General Household Surveys 1973 and 1985, HMSO, 1976 and 1987, tables 2.6 and 5.13
32. *BSA Bulletin* No. 53, January 1988, table 12
33. AMA, *Mortgage Arrears: Owner Occupiers at Risk*, 1986
34. *BSA Bulletin* No. 55, July 1988, table 17
35. DoE, Press Notice: *Homelessness Statistics, various issues*
36. Karn et al, 'Low income home ownership in the inner city', in Booth and Crook (eds), *Low Cost Home Ownership*, Gower, 1986
37. Ray Robinson, *Housing Economics and Public Policy*, MacMillan, 1979, pp.100-103.

CHAPTER **3**

Into the Future

The first part of this chapter describes and evaluates improvement policies in the private sector since 1979, and the second discusses the prospects for the 1990s in the light of the Government's completed review of the longer term aspects of these policies.

Improvement Policies since 1979

All governments have encouraged the repair and improvement of private sector housing. The chief method of achieving this aim has been to support voluntary activity by individual owners. Financial assistance is provided in the form of a grant which meets part of the cost of whatever building work is necessary. The present Government entered office in 1979 with a housing programme whose keystone was the promotion of wider opportunities for home ownership. The spearhead of this campaign was the sale of public sector homes through the Right To Buy and other initiatives. Over 750,000 have been sold, mostly to their tenants, in England in the last nine years.[1] The Government's initial interest in the problems of older private sector housing was not great.

Some stimulation of improvement activity was intended by minor changes to the grant system. The wider availability of grants for repair work only; the extension of the highest rates of grant to homes inside as well as outside statutory improvement areas; increased eligible costs and a greater flexibility on improvement standards were all included in a, largely uncontroversial, package of measures in the Housing Act of 1980. But these and similar initiatives had little immediate impact on the level of activity. This was largely because the Government put little extra money into any of the schemes.

In fact, any opportunity for progress was prevented by two successive reductions in authorised capital expenditure and a mid-1980 standstill on the letting of new construction contracts by local authorities. Gross capital spending allocations fell rapidly — by 43 per cent in real terms — in the two years to 1981.[2] Many authorities had little choice but to stop or reduce grant approvals in order to meet prior commitments.[3] But in the spring of 1982, the Government gave the green light for an increase in spending on improvement grants. In his budget statement, the Chancellor of the Exchequer announced that an extra £75 million could be spent by English authorities in support of improvement by private owners. More money was now available for grant assistance and the value of some grants was increased. Grants for major repairs, and for the provision of basic amenities, were made more attractive by increasing them to a maximum 90 per cent of the eligible cost, instead of the usual maximum 75 per cent. The Government was able to direct this additional cash into the improvement grant scheme by offering to pay the large part of any extra cost borne by individual authorities. The announcement meant that a rise of about 50 per cent in grant expenditure was possible above that of the previous year.[4]

The motives behind this decision were probably mixed. Officially the purpose was to encourage the use of spare capacity in the construction industry, which had been badly hit by the recession. But urban problems had been brought back into the political spotlight by the civil disturbances of 1981. By this time the preliminary, and no doubt unwelcome, results of the 1981 EHCS were known to the Department of the Environment. During 1981 a series of independent reports was published by professional institutes, local authority associations and pressure groups which all drew attention to the decline in activity and argued for extra resources to be devoted to the improvement programme.[5] In the light of these concerns, it became desirable to boost improvement activity; a decision, no doubt, made more attractive in the run-up to a general election.

Local authorities were later allowed to spend without limit on home improvement grants in the remainder of 1982/83 and the whole of 1983/84.[6] The 90 per cent grant offer was also extended to April 1984.[7] In December of 1982, the results of the 1981 EHCS were published. The Government was able to deflect a great deal of adverse comment by issuing a list of its recent improvement initiatives.[8]

The increase in capital allocations for grant expenditure by local authorities led to a boom in grant-aided improvement activity (**Table 9**).

The official line on improvement policy was amplified by John Stanley, the Housing Minister, in January 1983.

'As we start 1983, all the signs are that both new housing building and home improvements will be spearheads of economic recovery this year ... a veritable explosion in home improvement is now taking place, with expenditure on improvement more than doubling in the course of just one year'.[9]

The 'explosion' was in full swing during the election and peaked in 1984 when nearly 230,000 grants were paid to private owners and tenants — a record.

Table 9   Renovation Grants paid to Private Owners and Tenants, England[1] (thousands of dwellings/£million)

	Dwellings (thousands)				
	Conversion and Improvement	Intermediate and Special	Repairs	Total	Amount (£m)
1978	49.4	7.9	0.2	57.6	76.4
1979	57.2	7.8	0.3	65.4	100.2
1980	65.8	8.1	0.5	74.5	127.3
1981	49.1	14.7	5.1	68.9	148.2
1982	54.7	20.6	28.7	104.0	282.2
1983	79.5	27.2	113.1	219.8	655.5
1984	84.0	29.0	116.1	229.1	839.4
1985	53.0	29.0	54.4	136.4	525.1
1986	47.0	24.6	41.7	113.3	394.9
1987	48.9	20.2	41.3	110.4	367.7

Note: (1) Including grants paid to housing associations under private owner legislation.
Source: DoE, HCS 1976-1986
    DoE, HCS December Quarter 1987, Part 2 No.32, table 2.18
    DoE, Information Bulletin 309, 7 June 1988.

Effect of the 1982-84 Grant 'Explosion'

The likely impact of the boom in grant-aided activity between 1982 and 1984 can be gauged by comparing it with contemporary estimates of the minimum number of homes which needed attention in order to achieve an improvement in national housing conditions. Compared with the AMA's 1981 estimate of an annual programme of 150,000 grant-aided improved homes, it can be argued that the period represented a measurable change for the better with an average of 184,000 homes improved each year.[10] One reservation is that low cost intermediate and repair grants represented 60 per cent of grant approvals made during this period as against only 17 per cent in the previous three years. Longer term and more satisfactory conditions are generally achieved with more costly improvement grants which are usually targeted on the worst houses. Another qualification, advanced by Gibson, also needs to be taken into account. He suggests that the rapid expansion of grant approvals must have led to inadequate supervision of much of the building work by local authority staff and when this is combined with the re-emergence of 'cowboy builders', as the industry overheated, to a lot of dubious quality work. As a result, he suggests, many homes will require early remedial reimprovement.[11]

Another assessment of the potential impact of the boom can be made by looking at London. In the six years between the London house condition surveys of 1979 and 1985, there was no reduction in the number of private sector homes needing medium or expensive repairs **(Table 2)**.·But between 1979 and the peak year of 1984 the rate of grant approvals multiplied fivefold.[12] Between the two surveys over 120,000 improvement and repair grants were paid to London's private owners and tenants.[13] The 'explosion' seems to have done no more than stem the tide of disrepair in London.

It is unlikely, therefore, that the short-lived boom has had anything other than a marginal impact on private sector house conditions. When the 1986 EHCS is published later this year, its results will almost certainly show that little progress has been made in halting, let alone reversing, the rate of deterioration of private sector housing.

There is little published research to show who might have benefited from the boom. The limited information made available from a study *'The Distribution of Grant Enquiry (DGE)'* carried out by the DoE in 1983 fails to distinguish between grant recipients before and during the boom period. A similar study *'The Distribution of House Renovation Grants in Greater London'* carried out for the Greater London Council only looked at grant recipients after the boom was over.[14] Fortunately, a parallel study to the English DGE carried out by the Welsh Office does provide some data which allows a comparison to be made. It found that during the boom there was an increase of almost 60 per cent in the proportion of grants which went to elderly households (from 21 per cent to 33 per cent). The financial characteristics of recipients were also not the same after the increase in grant rates. The proportion who earned less than £4,000 per annum rose to nearly 50 per cent from 35 per cent.[15] The temporary relaxation of the usual limits clearly led to a greater take-up of grants by poorer households in Wales, even if at the same time it also led to more grants going to a lower proportion of better off people. It is very probable that events in England were similar.

The small changes made in 1980, and the special circumstances prevailing between 1982 and 1984, provided useful tools in building an improvement package to help many more grant applicants. But the expanded programme only lasted two years. Following the general election of 1983, the Government announced that the 90 per cent grant provisions would not be extended beyond April 1984 and a little later reduced the amount of money available to local authorities to spend on grants. Mr Gow, the new Housing Minister, said in October 1983 that:

'We will be concentrating the limited amount of taxpayers' money on those in greatest need. The maintenance and improvement of our housing stock is of the greatest long term importance for all of us. But taxpayers' money is not unlimited... The Government will do all it can, within the resources available, to provide opportunity and choice'.[16]

By 1986 grant approvals had fallen to half the 1984 level.

Private sector improvement was a prime target for cuts since expenditure had risen sharply, fuelled largely by receipts from council house sales. As these receipts began to fall, the pressure on the DoE to cut the programme rather than find replacement funds was great. The programme was also vulnerable to the criticism that it was not targeted accurately on needs. Many felt that it often subsidised work which would otherwise have been done by owners from their own resources.

Prospects for the 1990s

Housing has borne the brunt of public expenditure cuts since 1979. Its share of public spending has fallen from over 7 per cent in 1978/79 to under 4 per cent in 1988/89. Total spending fell from £6.4 billion to £2.5 billion over this period (1984/85 prices).[17] The distribution of housing spending between public and private sectors also changed considerably during this period. On top of the reduction in expenditure, there has been a transfer in the balance away from the public towards the private sector, transmitted by the improvement boom. The proportion of capital expenditure by local authorities on private sector improvement increased sevenfold between 1978/79 and 1984/85 — from 4 per cent to 28 per cent.[18] This shift impacted mainly on new building and slum clearance by local authorities. While public sector activity has declined sharply, speculative private development has not filled the gap (**Table 10**).

Expenditure on improvement has to be set against new build and clearance rates. The average age of private sector housing, excluding that bought under the Right to Buy, is increasing simply because it is being replaced at a lower rate than a decade ago. As housing ages its condition will worsen unless improvement spending rises to match the rate of deterioration.

During the 1980s the Government was able to reduce and reshape expenditure in line with the priority for home ownership. Specific Exchequer contributions were used which allowed local authorities to increase rapidly spending on grants at little extra cost to their ratepayers. The Government admitted that:

'These contributions have been used as a method of influencing authorities' spending patterns — particularly by increasing the level of support towards home improvement grants.'[19]

Table 10   New Build Completions and Slum Clearance, England (thousands of dwellings)

	New Build Completions			Dwellings Demolished or Closed[1]
	Public sector	Private sector	Total	
1978	113.9	127.5	241.4	38.9
1979	91.1	118.4	209.5	32.4
1980	94.1	110.0	204.1	28.7
1981	71.8	98.9	170.7	28.3
1982	42.6	108.0	150.7	23.8
1983	43.8	127.3	171.2	15.7
1984	43.3	136.6	179.9	11.2
1985	34.4	131.1	165.5	9.5
1986	29.6	141.3	170.9	8.6
1987	27.0	148.9	175.9	7.0

Note :(1) Financial not calendar year
Source: DoE, Information Bulletin 309, 7 June 1988.
    DoE, HCS December Quarter 1987, Part 2. No 32, Table 2.26

It was never the Government's intention that expenditure on grants should continue indefinitely at the levels of 1982 to 1984. Since it came into office, it has been committed to reining in public expenditure accompanied wherever possible by a relaxation of state regulation and control. It should be recalled that the grant explosion was financed, not by new money, but by council house sales. A direct link between general economic performance and improved housing conditions was a clear theme of government thinking. The Housing Minister said in 1983:

> 'The condition of the housing stock is not related simply to the amount of public funds available. Public expenditure can only prime the pump... One of the Government's tasks is to create a strong national economy where there is a steady and widespread rise in disposable incomes.'[20]

A stronger economy was the key to improved housing conditions in the private sector, not more intervention.

As the Government approached mid-term it became clearer how the inconsistency between an economic policy which stressed public expenditure savings and a housing policy which gave priority to home ownership would be resolved. The internal review of longer term improvement policy, initially begun in response to the 1981 EHCS, had been resumed after the general election. The balance to be struck in the future between the twin objectives of reducing spending and of encouraging private provision was finally embodied in the Green Paper '*Home Improvement: A New Approach*', published in May 1985.

The 1985 Green Paper

The premise underlying the Green Paper was that owners should carry the primary burden of maintaining and improving their homes while the government's role should be confined to creating an environment which encourages self-help. Intervention is justified in some circumstances, it added, but public funds should be spent in the most cost-effective way and directed to those who would not otherwise be able to carry out the necessary renovation work. The improvement grant scheme, it claimed, failed to target help where it was most needed and there was evidence that many of those eligible for grants could afford to finance work from their own resources or by borrowing.

The Green Paper proposed that direct support would in the future be limited to providing help for the poorest owners. Such help would only be available to bring homes up to a new standard of fitness. Eligibility for assistance would be determined by a test of the financial circumstances of the owner occupier's household. No similar test was proposed for private landlords. Discretionary grant aid for other essential works above the new standard would be replaced by loans which although interest free would be secured on an equity sharing basis. Area policies were endorsed but little more than adjustments to the practical arrangements were suggested.

The Green Paper proposals received a barrage of criticism from local authorities, professional bodies and pressure groups. SHAC was one of nineteen signatories to a letter to the Secretary of State for the Environment which urged the Government to reconsider its proposals. (**Appendix Two**). The Green Paper's transparent objectives were to reduce public expenditure by substituting the maximum possible use of private funds and to target whatever resources remained more effectively. Since the private sector has not filled the gap left by the decline in new house building by local authorities, it is unrealistic to imagine that it could replace a similar gap left by the withdrawal of public spending on improvement. The Government's analysis ignored the fact that most households in the poorest stock are also those least likely to benefit from a recovery in Britain's economic fortunes. The limited information available from the Green Paper supported few of its assertions, nor did it facilitate an evaluation of the proposals. The proposals are unlikely to arrest the decay of private sector housing and the fear is that the rate of decline will accelerate if they are implemented in their present form. The key to solving the problems of the older housing stock is more investment by both public and private sectors. The Government's plans will reduce the former and discourage the latter. Increased spending along with greater incentives and more flexible forms of intervention are all needed if the backlog of disrepair is to be tackled successfully. The Green Paper was a missed opportunity, and left only a gloomy prognosis for the future health of the nation's housing.

It did, oddly enough, represent a novel confirmation of the logic of owner occupation. Financial assistance for improvement (although not yet for acquisition) is seemingly inconsistent with a philosophy which sees the tenure as encouraging independence and self-reliance. Freedom from state control also means freedom from state help.

The 1987 White Paper

Little more was heard of the Green Paper proposals until the general election campaign of 1987. The Conservative manifesto promised, *inter alia*, that a future government would introduce a better targeted improvement grant scheme.[21] A few months after its return to office the Government released a White Paper '*Housing: The Government's Proposals*' which set out the main strands of its policy over the life of the new Parliament.[22] It would continue to encourage the growth of home ownership, and introduce measures to revive the moribund private rented sector and to reduce the role of local authorities as providers of housing. The 1985 proposals on home improvement policy resurfaced, although the equity sharing loans concept had been dropped. A consultation paper explaining the detailed aspects of the proposals, and the mechanisms for implementing them, appeared a month later. Legislation is expected shortly, but it is unlikely that the new proposals could be brought into effect before April 1990.[23]

Summary

The grant 'boom' of 1982 to 1984 was not sustained when the evidence is that it should have been. The expanded programme may have resulted in a marginal improvement in the condition of private sector housing. Public spending on housing has fallen substantially over the last decade. House building performance and slum clearance activity are below the levels of the 1970s. This means that the existing stock is ageing. As it ages its condition will worsen unless improvement spending rises to match the rate of deterioration. The problems of older housing point to the need for a reappraisal of existing policies and programmes. Increased spending, greater incentives and more effective intervention are all required. The Government's plans will lead to reduced public investment, do little to encourage increased activity by private owners and fail to address the problems revealed by the 1981 EHCS.

References

1. DoE, HCS 1976-1986, table 9.6
2. Phil Leather and Alan Murie, 'The decline in public expenditure', p.32 in *The Housing Crisis* (ed. Peter Malpass), Croom Helm, 1986
3. Mike Gibson, 'Housing renewal: privatisation and beyond', p.106, ibid
4. DoE Press Notice 91, 16 March 1982
5. Royal Town Planning Institute, *Renewal of Older Housing Areas: Into the Eighties*, 1981; Institution of Environmental Health Officers, *Area Improvement*, 1981; AMA, *Ruin or Renewal: Choices for Our Ageing Housing* 1981; and SHAC, *Good Housekeeping: An Examination of Housing Repair and Improvement Policy*, 1981
6. DoE Press Notices 491 and 28, 14 December 1982 and 28 January 1983
7. DoE Press Notice 358, 5 October 1982
8. DoE Press Notice 493, 14 December 1982
9. DoE Press Notice 7, 12 January 1983
10. AMA, *Ruin or Renewal: Choices for Our Ageing Housing*, 1981
11. Gibson, op cit, p.107
12. DoE, HCS 1976-1986, HMSO, table 7.4
13. Hansard, Written Answer, Cols 228-230, 20 November 1985
14. Green Paper, 1985, Annex I — Distribution of Grant Enquiries. Thames Polytechnic, *The Distribution of House Renovation Grants in Greater London*, Greater London Council, 1986. (London DGE, 1986)
15. Welsh Office, *Survey of House Renovation Grants: Wales* 1983/84, HMSO, 1985, table 34
16. DoE Press Notice 445, 20 October 1983
17. HM Treasury, The Government's Expenditure Plans 1986-87 to 1988-89 Cmnd. 9702, 1986, Chart 1.11 and table 2.2
18. Phil Leather, op cit, p.42
19. Green Paper, 1985, para. 77
20. DoE Press Notice 445, 20 October 1983
21. Conservative Central Office, *The Next Moves Forward: The Conservative Manifesto* 1987, p.12
22. White Paper, 1987
23. DoE/Welsh Office. *Home Improvement Policy: the Government's Proposals*, DoE, November 1987. (Consultation Paper, 1987)

Home Improvement Grants

The first part of this chapter looks at the current grant system and its limitations, the second at the Government's proposed changes and the third suggests an alternative approach.

Introduction

Grants to private owners for the improvement of their homes have been available in their present form since the 1940s. The rationale for grants is that by lowering the price of improvement work a much greater quantity will be undertaken than would otherwise occur. The trend has been for the scope of the grant system to be gradually extended: most recently in early 1988.[1] The success of improvement policy, especially in the owner occupied sector, is reliant on the participation and co-operation of individual owners. In practice, this means that voluntary grant take-up is the single most important method of achieving progress. Almost all improvement activity, whether grant assisted or not, is undertaken by owners voluntarily. In 1984 only 5 per cent of all grants paid were mandatory following the use by local authorities of their powers to order repairs to a private sector home.[2]

Current Grant System

The need for direct financial assistance to low-income owners is supported by successive house condition surveys. Households living in poor housing conditions have, on average, lower incomes than those who live in homes in reasonable repair. This is most marked for those in the worst housing — properties which are unfit or lack basic amenities — where the proportion of elderly households is high. Forty per cent of the owner occupiers of houses judged unfit would need to find a sum of more than three times their annual income to put them into reasonable condition (see **Table 7**).

For such households there is little or no prospect of funding improvement or repair work by saving or borrowing. If importance is attached to bringing the worst housing up to a decent standard, then public sector financial support will inevitably have to provide a considerable part of the cost. How successful is the existing system at reaching the worst properties and the poorest households?

Results from the 1983 DGE show that grants generally go to homes with low market values. This was partly because of their type: the majority are small terraced houses built before 1919, as well as their condition. 70 per cent of them had rateable values below £150. Improvement grants concentrated on the worst houses; 40 per cent went to unfit dwellings; 60 per cent to dwellings with repair costs in excess of £7,000 and half to dwellings lacking at least one amenity.[3] In London 82 per cent of grants went to homes built before 1919 and 68 per cent to terraced houses.[4] So grants are reasonably well targeted on the worst condition properties.

The 1983 DGE, and in so far as it picked up recipients the 1981 EHCS, enable comparisons to be drawn between the population who received grants and those people who according to the 1981 EHCS were potential grant recipients. Only 7 per cent of grants went to private tenanted homes whereas 27 per cent of the worst condition stock is rented privately. Only 2 per cent of grants were received by unemployed households. A fifth of recipients were retired owner occupiers compared with one third found to be living in potentially grant aidable homes. Elderly single person households received 5 per cent of grants but 19 per cent were potentially eligible for one.

Because elderly and unemployed households were under-represented among grant recipients, the average income of recipients was about £7,000 (1982 prices), about the same as the then national average, but substantially higher than potential recipients whose average household income was £3,380 (1981 prices).[5] 27 per cent of London households occupying unsatisfactory housing had incomes of less than £50 per week in 1985, but only 13 per cent of grant recipients had incomes below this level.[6] Grant recipients are not too dissimilar from potential recipients in terms of their socio-economic group. The 1983 DGE did not reveal any group which was significantly over or under represented, although the proportion of professional and managerial households who received grants was lower than the proportion potentially eligible.[7]

Although the current scheme has no formal test of an applicant's resources it is not as badly targeted as might be supposed, either in terms of

Table 11   **Characteristics of Households in Dwellings with Grant Potential and of Grant Recipients, 1981-83, England (% of households and recipients)**

	Grant Potential	Grant Recipients
Household Head Unemployed	5	2
Household Head Retired	33	20
Elderly Single Person Household	19	5
Household Income under £3,381 pa	53	24
Professional/Employers/Managers	18	13
Private Tenanted Dwelling	27	7

Source: EHCS, 1983, tables 58 and 59
        Green Paper, 1985, Annex 1, Figure 1

homes or households. Certainly there is scope for improvement. Grants fail to reach as many poorer households as they should. But this is not because better-off people are getting a disproportionate amount of help. The 1983 DGE results suggest that suspicions about major abuses of the scheme are unfounded. It is clear, nonetheless, that many of those on low incomes, especially the elderly, are reluctant to apply for a grant.[8] One explanation for this is that grants do not provide enough help to poorer households.

Amount of Grant Available

There is often an inverse relationship between the cost of essential work to a house and the financial resources of its occupiers. The grant system does not satisfactorily cope with this, because the amount of grant available is more closely related to the condition of a property than it is to the circumstances of the occupying household. This mismatch was clearly demonstrated by the 1981 EHCS. As part of its analysis the cost of installing amenities and carrying out necessary repairs was computed for each sample dwelling and offset against potential grant assistance at the appropriate rate. The resulting 'grant gap' was then matched against household income. This exercise revealed that, even with grant aid, most households in the poorer stock would be left with a sum to find, and for many this would be substantial. A third of those living in the very worst stock would still need to find an amount equivalent to more than three times their gross annual income.

Table 12   'Grant Gap' as a Proportion of Annual Income (Owner Occupiers only), 1981, England (% of households)

	Satisfactory Dwellings	Unfit Dwellings	Unfit and in Serious Disrepair
0 — 100%	97	75	47
101% — 300%	3	11	21
301% or more	0	14	32

Note: Gross Household Income
Source: EHCS, 1983, tables L and 30

There are three linked reasons for this 'grant gap' or shortfall in assistance. Not all work carried out is considered eligible for assistance, actual costs frequently exceed maximum allowable costs and grants themselves cover only a proportion of the allowable costs. Consequently the maximum rate of grant of 90 per cent, given in a few cases of hardship, implies very much more than a 10 per cent contribution by the owner. On average, improvement and intermediate grants contribute less than 60 per cent of the total cost of the necessary work.[9] In London, the proportions are even lower. Improvement grants cover on average 50 per cent of costs and intermediate grants only 43 per cent. This left the typical applicant for an improvement grant in London with over £7,000 to find.[10] Many poor households are simply unable to bridge the gap between the total cost of the remedial work and the amount of grant available. The result is that they cannot take up a grant.

Lack of awareness about grants is yet another reason for low take-up. The 1981 EHCS found that around a quarter of households in unsatisfactory dwellings had not heard of grants: they tended to be tenants or older people; older women in particular. But over half of those who had heard of grants had not even considered applying for one.[11]

Complexity of the System

Another drawback of the grant system is its complexity which makes it difficult for people to know whether they are eligible or not, as well as adding to the administrative costs incurred by local authorities.

There are four separate types of grant, each available for a different range of work, although there are substantial overlaps.

☐   **Intermediate Grants** — for installing missing standard amenities and associated repairs. These grants are mandatory.

☐ **Repairs Grants** — for substantial and structural repairs to pre-1919 houses. They are normally discretionary unless a local authority has served a repairs notice.

☐ **Improvement Grants** — for major improvements to houses or for conversions. Allowable costs can include a substantial proportion of repairs. Improvement grants are always discretionary.

☐ **Special Grants** — for houses in multiple occupation. For installing standard amenities and/or means of escape from fire plus associated repairs. They are discretionary unless a local authority has served an appropriate notice.

Despite this plurality, the range of grant-aidable work is not comprehensive. It is not possible to get a grant for repairs alone to a house built after 1919, though repairs to the same house can be grant-aided at the same time as improvements. The system automatically accords a higher priority to the provision of an inside wc in a house with a sound roof than to the repair of a leaking roof. Owner occupiers, but not landlords, cannot usually get an improvement or a repairs grant if their home has a rateable value above £225 (£400 in London). Grant rates vary between a usual minimum of 50 per cent and a maximum of 90 per cent of the allowable cost depending on the nature of the work being carried out, the location of the dwelling and the circumstances of the applicant. Allowable costs also vary in a similar way. It was estimated in 1981 that the four types of grant, plus the separate thermal insulation grant, together with the different cost limits and rates produced ninety different variations of grant aid.[12]

The rateable value limits act as a proxy for a means-test. There are about 3.7 million homes whose condition, other things being equal, would make them eligible for a grant. But 0.6 million fall outside the rateable value limits. The 1981 EHCS found that the limits did have some justification as a means test in that the 'excluded' households had double the average income of the 'included'. But the range of incomes within each group was large and overlapping, and almost 30 per cent of the excluded group had incomes below the median of the eligible group.[13]

The age restriction on repairs grants excluded an additional 0.35 million homes. It was imposed as recently as 1980 when repairs grants, previously only available in Housing Action Areas, were made more widely available so that priority could be given to the oldest housing. But the condition of the excluded stock, particularly that built between the wars, is showing distinct signs of worsening and a great deal is occupied by poorer households.[14] The Green Paper estimated that up to 150,000 owner occupiers ineligible for help under the rateable value and age restrictions could not afford any of the essential work to their homes.[15]

Two major criticisms can be made about the current grant system. First, it does not give enough help to low-income households. Consequently they are unable to take up grants. Second, it is over-complex and difficult to understand. The eligibility criteria exclude many homes which are in an unsatisfactory condition. The system needs to be redesigned to focus assistance on the worst condition properties and to tailor the amount of assistance more closely to individual circumstances.

Government's Proposed Changes

The Government's proposals were initially revealed in the 1985 Green Paper and restated, with minor changes, in the 1987 White Paper. A single form of mandatory grant will replace the present four types of grant. It will be available for any improvement or repair work necessary to bring a property up to a new standard of fitness. Above this standard grant assistance would remain at the discretion of local authorities. Rateable value limits as a test of eligibility will cease to be used, and the Government is considering replacing age restrictions with more flexible arrangements.

Grant entitlement will in future be determined by a test of household resources. This test will take into account the cost of the work required, and the household's ability to finance it from income and savings. The test would be compatible with that used for the housing benefit scheme on the grounds of 'consistency' and 'simplicity'. Households with a net income below an unspecified threshold would be entitled to assistance with the full cost of the eligible work. Grant aid would then be progressively reduced on a single sliding scale as income rose above this threshold. At an, again unspecified, level of net income grant entitlement would be nil. For private landlords entitlement will take account of their ability to finance the work from rental income.[16]

Assessment

The proposal to make entitlement to, and the amount of, a grant dependent on a means-test has received much adverse comment. To link it to housing benefit would suggest a very low threshold of entitlement to assistance. A couple, one working, with two children paying the average local authority rates of £7.70 per week cease to qualify for any housing benefit at a gross income level of about £124 per week — approximately half the average weekly earnings for such households. A pensioner paying the average local authority rates, in this case £6.40 per week, does not get any housing benefit if gross income rises above £69 per week.[17] A pensioner only gets the maximum help with rates through the housing benefit scheme if his or her income is at or below £44.05 per week. The 1981 EHCS found that only a quarter of the owner occupiers of unsatisfactory homes, who would need to find three or more times their annual income to pay for remedial works, were actually getting a rate rebate.[18]

The eligibility limits for housing benefit are already so low, that using the scheme to assess entitlement to a grant would inevitably exclude many people who could not fund all or most of the work from their own resources. Most of those who did qualify could afford to make little or no contribution of their own. Yet only the very poorest would not be expected to make a contribution.

There are other objections to a means-tested scheme. Take-up of any benefit which depends on a claimant providing detailed proof of need before assistance is given is always low. Take-up of housing benefit by owner occupiers was recently estimated to be as low as 64 per cent.[19] A means-test is very likely to reinforce any reluctance to apply for a grant. A means-test is also a 'snapshot' of an applicant's resources at a moment in time. While this may be appropriate when assessing weekly living costs, it is hardly so for decisions which may fix the quality of someone's housing for years into the future. It is also questionable whether it is appropriate to assess a household's resources rather than the owner's alone. Although it is generally expected that all members of a family should contribute to its living expenses, this does not normally include spending on repairs and improvements.

Even more worrying is the plan to base the means-test on that used for housing benefit. This scheme is notoriously complex. The test of resources for the revised scheme introduced last April is much more complicated than that which it replaced. The housing benefit thresholds, above which grant will eventually taper off to zero, are not based on an objective assessment of need but on what the Government thinks the country can afford. They are also very complicated in that they comprise a basic personal allowance (of which there are seven variations), four different additions for children (depending on age) together with a combination of one or more of twelve different premiums which take into account special circumstances such as age, family status and disability. This structure means, for example, that a pensioner aged, say 78, would receive a lower amount of grant assistance, than a pensioner of over 80 years. A family with a child aged 16 would get more grant than a family in similar circumstances with a child aged 15. Whatever justification there is for giving similar households different amounts of housing benefit, there appears to be little when deciding the amount of grant they would receive.

The precise impact of these changes on the level of grant-aided improvement is impossible to quantify at this stage. It is not possible to estimate how many owner occupiers currently eligible for a grant would not qualify under the means-test proposals. But it seems probable that the number of homes improved with the help of a grant will decline. Fewer owners will qualify and many of those who do will receive a lower amount of assistance. A crude assessment can be made however.

About 1.6 million owner occupiers are currently eligible for a grant.[20] Removal of the eligibility criteria may increase this to between 2.2-2.4 million. But grant entitlement would depend on how many of them had a low enough income in relation to improvement costs to qualify for assistance. If entitlement is based on the housing benefit scheme it is extremely doubtful whether many more than 1 million would qualify. And only a proportion of those who qualified (perhaps a third) would get assistance with the full cost of the work. It could be even worse. The 1985 GLHCS found that only 13 per cent of the owner occupiers of unsatisfactory accommodation in London were getting a means-tested social security benefit including housing benefit.[21] A reliable estimate will have to await the results of the 1986 EHCS and the release by the Government of the figures for its home improvement thresholds.

The proposed means-tested scheme might effectively exclude better-off people but the likelihood that it will lead to reduced spending on grants and discourage private investment and the possibility that it would deter many eligible households from even applying for a grant, hardly adds up to a convincing argument in its favour. There is no direct link between entitlement to housing benefit and a need for an improvement grant. A means-test would add further complications and anomalies to an already complex scheme, when the aim should be simplification. It is doubtful whether the housing benefit scheme can be successfully adapted to assess entitlement to an improvement grant.

The real failure of the proposals is that they confuse two distinct issues. First, there is the question of whether grants simply provide too great a subsidy to better-off households. Although some could undoubtedly afford to carry out the work from their own resources, the DGE results show that grants are not as badly targeted as might be supposed. Second, there is the question of whether grants offer an effective stimulus to poorer households who would not otherwise have done the work. The evidence is that they do not, but the Government does not satisfactorily address this issue. Withdrawing assistance from the better-off is *not* the same as extending it to poorer households. The proposals significantly do not commit the Government to redirect any savings produced from a means-tested scheme to the most needy households. Neither is there any real sign of a determination to ensure that such households actually receive the assistance to which they are entitled. In the last analysis a means-tested scheme can only add to the existing deterrents to home improvement.

There are arguments against restricting grants only to comparatively poor households. Private owners lack sufficient financial incentives to maintain and improve their homes. The housing market under-values improvement expenditure: a phenomenon independent of the resources of the individual owner. But it is in the national interest that the private sector stock is kept in reasonable repair. Grant assistance can be justified where the eventual economic and social cost of not carrying out renovation work is greater than the public expenditure costs associated with encouraging earlier renewal. The expense of replacing run-down housing is great, while the social consequences of a return to 1950s and 60s-style clearance and redevelopment are grave. Grants, then, have an economic role in minimising the potential waste of public resources arising from the neglect and decay of houses which still have useful life left in them.

A New Renovation Grant Scheme

Simplification of the existing system is a long overdue measure and one that SHAC has advocated for some time. The introduction of a single type of grant to replace the present four is a positive step forward as is the proposal to make grants mandatory if a property is below the fitness standard. The plan to abolish rateable value limits and relax age restrictions focuses assistance on the worst properties. Rateable values are an inadequate test of ability to pay and the limits do exclude a substantial number of poor households.

Improvement and intermediate grants are normally available only for homes built before 1961, or before 1919 in the case of a repairs grant. The former restriction is justified because the Building Regulations have ensured that homes built after 1961 are of good standard and include all the standard amenities. Given the evidence of disrepair in some post-1919 housing, particularly that built between the wars, it would be sensible to relax this limit. Furthermore, it would complicate a unitary grant scheme, divided only between mandatory and discretionary elements, if some works were given a different cut-off date than others. It would appear sensible to opt for a cut-off date of 1961 for all types of work although it might, for practical reasons, have to be phased in progressively.

The proposed new fitness standard includes the standard amenities which does away with the need for a separate mandatory grant for this purpose. However, the new standard is deficient in several respects and needs revision. Housing standards are examined later in *Chapter 8*.

If a property is judged unfit, local authorities have powers to compel the owner to carry out the work necessary to bring it up to a good standard of repair. Such powers are normally used against private landlords, not owner occupiers. If a local authority has issued a notice requiring repairs to a property, it has also to provide a grant to the owner (irrespective of its rateable value). If there is a case for awarding a grant following compulsory action, it would seem illogical to withhold a mandatory grant applied for voluntarily. There is also a case for making grants mandatory in statutory improvement areas. Not only do local authorities have tougher compulsory powers in such areas, but the success of an area depends on securing the improvement of a very high proportion of its unsatisfactory houses. Withholding a grant from the middle income households living in such areas would run the risk of seriously impeding progress, particularly if they occupied homes in critical locations. The only way a local authority could, in the absence of grants, tackle such properties would be by compulsory purchase which would be even more costly. Where there are powers to compel the improvement of individual unfit houses and to tackle areas of unsatisfactory houses it must be appropriate to offer some grant assistance, whatever the financial circumstances of the occupiers.

Discretionary assistance for homes which are above the minimum standard and outside a statutory improvement area should continue to be available. Market forces alone will not be sufficient to secure the improvement of all such homes, or even to prevent the further deterioration of many, without the inducement of a grant.

Grant rates should reflect the circumstances of the applicant, subject to a higher minimum rate of grant being available to households occupying unfit properties or living in a statutory improvement area where there are sufficient benefits to the wider community to justify more generous support. Mandatory grants should be available at a minimum rate of, say, 75 per cent, and discretionary at a minimum rate of 50 per cent. Both discretionary and mandatory grants should be available at a higher rate for those in financial hardship. There is a simple, practical alternative to a means-test to determine eligibility for the higher rate of grant. This is to base it on *'passporting'* — making automatically eligible those in certain groups already identified by their entitlement to other forms of state support. Households in receipt of income support, family credit or housing benefit should certainly qualify. So should those getting a long-term national insurance benefit such as a retirement pension or invalidity benefit. Local authorities could be given discretion to award a higher rate in other circumstances which they felt were appropriate. This method would include the great majority of households who might have difficulty in meeting any of the cost of the work and exclude most who could afford some or all of it while at the same time avoiding a complex, time-consuming and wasteful means-test. The higher rate for mandatory grants should meet 100 per cent of allowable costs. Discretionary grants present more of a problem. The amount of assistance above the minimum rate could be left to the discretion of individual local authorities, but this might lead to inconsistency and unfairness. On balance, SHAC favours the present method under which those on low incomes are entitled to a maximum grant of 90 per cent of allowable costs.

Successive governments have failed to link allowable cost ceilings, known as eligible expense limits (EELs), to rises in building costs. They were fixed in 1983 but it was not until March 1988 that the Government proposed to raise them.[22] The irregular revision of EELs creates difficulties because over time less and less of the work necessary to bring a property up to standard qualifies for grant assistance. The AMA has also pointed out that EELs do not adequately reflect regional variations in building costs and bear no relation to either the size or the type of property concerned.[23] The Government suggested that one option for the future would be to have no EELs in the case of grants for unfit dwellings, and, on balance, SHAC favours this solution.[24] This would mean that those in receipt of the higher rate of mandatory grant, provided it was given to make their home fit, would get help with the full cost of the work. Retaining a limit for both mandatory and discretionary grants to properties above the fitness standard has greater validity provided it is index-linked to reflect changes in building costs.

Summary

The grant system is in need of overhaul, as is now accepted by the Government. It is not as effective as it could be in preserving the stock or in reflecting individual needs. It excludes some houses in poor condition and fails to offer sufficient help to those who need it most. The various criteria, conditions, limits and restrictions, whatever their original justification, make the system unnecessarily complex, cumbersome and hard to grasp.

The Government's planned changes go a long way towards simplifying the system but the means-test proposal is a retrograde measure. A unitary grant which is mandatory for any work to bring a property up to the standard of fitness is an overdue reform. Basing the means-test on the housing benefit scheme is particularly damaging because it would introduce new anomalies and complexities into the grant system.

SHAC's alternative proposal is that all households should remain eligible for a grant irrespective of their income falling on one side or another of an arbitrary threshold. Grant rates should however reflect the relative priority accorded to the necessary work and the circumstances of the applicant. The minimum rate of mandatory grant should be set at 75 per cent with a maximum 100 per cent for households identified by their receipt of a specified social security benefit. Discretionary grants should be available at a lower minimum rate of 50 per cent with a maximum of 90 per cent. For work to make a property fit the allowable cost should be equal to the actual cost. There should be a single cut-off date of 1961 for all types of work although it may have to be phased in gradually.

References

1. A grant designed to help with the costs of repairing and improving the common parts of buildings containing flats, such as roofs and staircases, which lie outside the flats themselves was introduced in February 1988. DoE News Release 96, 17 February 1988
2. Hansard, Written Answer, 26 November 1986, Col. 262
3. Green Paper, 1985, Annex I, paras. 7-8
4. London DGE, 1986, tables 12 and 14

5. Green Paper, 1985, Annex 1, para. 3
6. GLHCS, 1987, table 3.20.
    London DGE, 1986, table 36
7. Green Paper 1985, Annex 1, Figure 1
8. Green Paper, 1985, para. 27
9. Green Paper, 1985, para. 11
10. London DGE, 1986, table 50
11. EHCS, 1983, paras 7.4 — 7.5
12. Royal Town Planning Institute, *Renewal of Older Housing Areas: Into the Eighties,*
    1981, p.22
13. EHCS, 1983, para. 5.7 and table R
14. EHCS, 1983, table R
15. Green Paper, 1985, para. 27
16. Green Paper, 1985, paras. 26-42
    White Paper, 1987, paras. 2.17-2.18
    Consultation Paper, 1987, paras. 4-6 and 13-22.
17. Hansard, Written Answer, 24 March 1988, Cols. 216-217.
18. EHCS, 1983, table J
19. DHSS (Statistics and Research Division), Technical Note, Housing Benefit Take-Up
    1984, May 1987, table 2.
20. EHCS, 1983, table 57
21. GLHCS, 1987, table 3.36 (3)
22. DoE News Release 164, 17 March 1988
23. AMA, *Less Ruin: More Renewal*, 1986, para. 4.6
24. Consultation Paper, 1987, para. 24

5

Area Improvement

The first part of this chapter looks at the framework for and achievements of area improvement, the second discusses the potential for area-based policies, and the third assesses the Government's plans and suggests an alternative approach.

Introduction

The aim of area improvement, in contrast to the renovation of individual houses, is to halt the processes of housing and environmental decay in areas which contain concentrations of bad housing and help set them on the path of regeneration. From a modest beginning in the mid-1960s, policies attempting to focus attention and resources on a defined area have played an increasingly important role. Under present arrangements there are two types of statutory improvement area; a General Improvement Area (GIA) and a Housing Action Area (HAA). The main characteristics of each are set out below.

Types of Improvement Area

A typical GIA is aimed at encouraging largely voluntary action in a predominantly owner occupied area containing basically sound housing capable of being improved to a good standard. The environment should also offer scope for improvement. The average number of houses within a GIA is about 320.[1] Declaration itself should induce confidence but more specific measures to encourage residents to improve their homes include: a higher rate of grant (65 per cent) than the normal 50 per cent, and local authorities can carry out or assist with environmental works such as landscaping, the provision of open spaces or children's play areas. Authorities are also encouraged to improve the external appearance of buildings within GIAs and to provide new community facilities. Local authorities receive special Exchequer contributions to help with the cost of environmental works. Although the emphasis within GIAs is on voluntary action, authorities also have wide compulsory powers to deal with housing where encouragement alone has not proved sufficient. They are able to acquire land compulsorily and can pursue compulsory improvement of private rented housing on their own initiative. GIAs are not time limited.

A HAA on the other hand is designed to bring about the rapid improvement of unsatisfactory housing in areas where physical and social factors interact to create housing stress. Relevant factors include overcrowding, a high proportion of private rented accommodation and of households sharing facilities and a concentration of elderly and/or ethnic minority households. An average HAA consists of about 340 houses.[2] HAAs were first introduced in 1975 and are time limited with a normal life of five years extendable, with DoE approval, to a maximum of seven. This is to prompt authorities to get their programmes underway quickly and achieve results in a relatively short period.

A HAA, like a GIA, should itself create confidence among residents and act as a stimulus to voluntary improvement. But since housing conditions are normally worse than those found in a GIA, the inducement to private owners to improve their homes is greater. The maximum rate of improvement grant is normally 75 per cent, and this may be increased to 90 per cent where the applicant is deemed to suffer from hardship. Rateable value limits are waived in HAAs. Environmental powers are similar to those in GIAs, as are the compulsory improvement powers. Acquisition powers are wider and private landlords must inform the local authority when issuing a notice to quit or disposing of tenanted property. The purpose is to permit the local authority to assess the impact on the tenants and take whatever action is appropriate.

Since 1982 local authorities have been able to undertake 'envelope schemes' in HAAs. Enveloping is aimed at houses which existing policies have missed; basically sound private sector properties which their owners have failed to improve with grants for financial or other reasons. The central feature of enveloping is that the local authority organises and undertakes all the necessary repairs to the external fabric of a block or terrace of houses at no cost to the owners. By early 1987, 63 schemes had been completed, with another 43 in progress, together covering about 10,500 homes. Over half have been completed by just two authorities: Birmingham and Leicester.[3] Enveloping allows work on a large scale to be carried out to a high standard to a reasonable time scale. The visual impact can be dramatic. An owner's contribution to the cost of improvement is reduced to a level more in keeping with their ability to pay and makes further grant-aided work a viable and more worthwhile proposition. Research undertaken in Birmingham, which pioneered enveloping, suggests that its schemes have boosted optimism among residents and encouraged new private investment. It also found that enveloping is more likely to benefit existing, rather than new, residents compared with traditional HAAs and to stabilise community and tenure patterns. Doubts have been expressed about whether enveloping is rather too indiscriminate a subsidy and its cost relative to the usual approach. It is, in effect, a 100 per cent grant for external repair. But a growing awareness of the problems experienced by low-income owner occupiers often justifies this form of help whilst the cost is less than the alternative of municipalisation.[4]

A similar technique is to group individual repair grants into a single contract. Several authorities, such as Rochdale and Walsall, have adopted this approach, known as 'block repair'. It is suitable for small contracts on selected, difficult blocks and has the advantage of not being limited to HAAs. Envelope and block schemes are now recognised as tools of area implementation rather than policies in their own right. They are better suited to dealing with more deep-seated problems but both still retain the flexibility for subsequent voluntary internal improvement.

Progress and Potential for Area Improvement

Since 1975 about 164,000 private sector homes in both GIAs and HAAs have been improved with the help of a grant, representing 13 per cent of all grant-aided renovations.[5] At present there are 617,000 houses in improvement areas in England in 311 HAAs and 1,616 GIAs.[6]

An assessment of activity within areas alone is dependent on the date of declaration and the proportion of houses considered to be a target for renovation. The 1981 EHCS estimated that since 1976 18 per cent of properties within GIAs, and 19 per cent in HAAs had been improved.[7] A higher proportion is obtained if action is considered in terms of 'target' dwellings; that is excluding public sector improvements and houses already in a satisfactory condition. Between 1975 and 1980, 37 per cent of 'target' dwellings were improved within HAAs. National averages do, however, conceal wide variations in particular areas ranging from instances where virtually nothing had been achieved to others where almost complete improvement had taken place.[8]

The impact of area improvement depends to a considerable extent on public sector activity. Between 1975 and 1986, 57 per cent of all homes improved in HAAs had been improved by either local authorities or housing associations.[9]

In evaluating the contribution of area improvement it is important to separate performance within areas from their contribution to improving the national housing stock. Most GIAs and HAAs were effective to some degree;

only a minority were clearly failures. Three main reasons for lack of achievement in particular areas have been identified. Some were areas more suitable
for clearance than improvement. Low levels of grant take-up inhibited progress in others. In other cases, there was a clear lack of effort and commitment of resources by the local authority. However, area improvement has yet
to make a significant contribution to improving housing conditions on a national scale. In national terms, it is not the rate of progress within individual
areas which counts, but its relationship to the number of areas declared. The
small number of declarations, particularly of HAAs, has meant that too few
houses have been renovated.

The 1981 EHCS found that there is still considerable scope for area
action. The surveyors reckoned that about 1.4 million houses were in potential GIAs and HAAs not programmed for area improvement, representing about
three-quarters of all such houses.

**Table 13   Progress and Potential for Area Improvement, 1981, England
(thousands of dwellings)**

	Declared Areas	Proposed Areas	Prospective Areas
GIAs	411	150	1,120
HAAS	172	60	290
Total	583	210	1,410

Source: EHCS, 1983, table W

The 1981 EHCS found that decay into serious disrepair was significant
within proposed and prospective areas, but even within declared areas the proportion of houses in serious disrepair had remained more or less static. Although
improvement activity in areas has made an impact on housing conditions, this
is offset by the deterioration of houses not subject to action. Thus, despite
the success of many individual areas, the net result was no overall improvement in housing conditions.[10] The position was even worse in non-declared
areas. Serious disrepair in prospective HAAs doubled between 1976 and 1981
to account for almost a third of the stock. In fact, conditions had worsened
to such an extent in prospective HAAs that they were approaching those found
in clearance areas. The poor physical condition of houses within prospective
HAAs is paralleled by a social profile also close to that of clearance areas.
Under 40 per cent of heads of household were in full-time work and a high
proportion of residents were retired or elderly. Almost a half of all households
had incomes of £50 per week or less.[11]

Table 14 Trends in Serious Disrepair of Dwellings in Statutory Areas, England (% of dwellings)

Area action in 1981	Dwellings in Serious Disrepair	
	at previous survey	at present survey
GIAs:		
declared	13	14
proposed	4	12
prospective	10	17
HAAs:		
declared	22	24
proposed	18	20
prospective	15	31

Source: EHCS, 1983, table Y

Area policies have not yet succeeded in reversing housing decay. At best, the condition of houses within declared areas has deteriorated less rapidly than that of houses outside areas. Fewer HAAs have been declared than was originally anticipated. These facts have led to the questioning of the benefits of an area approach to housing renewal. It is not self-evident that improvement of the older stock is best pursued by the designation of small areas of bad housing for concentrated attention over a short period of time as opposed to a more general allocation of public resources to help owners improve their homes wherever they are located.

A Role for Area Improvement

A number of arguments can be advanced against an area approach. Two stand out. First, there are more houses in need of renovation outside areas than within them, so an area approach discriminates against the majority of houses and households in need. Declared and proposed areas contained 15 per cent of all unfit houses and some 11 per cent of those in serious disrepair. Prospective areas contained nearly a half and just over a third of these conditions respectively. Moreover, the growing incidence of disrepair is much less suited to an area approach. Only a quarter of homes needing repairs costing over £2,500 are within potential areas. And most areas contain houses which do not merit priority attention but which will receive it merely by virtue of their location.[12]

Second, evidence about the geographical concentration of poor physical conditions is only one component of a deeper critique of area policies. It has been suggested that social deprivation is not as dense as is assumed and that most people in need live outside small, localised areas. Furthermore, even if priority areas could be identified, conventional programmes rather than area-based ones might prove a better way of concentrating help on the poor and disadvantaged. Area policies imply that the causes of problems lie within such areas and are in some way capable of local solution. They thus focus attention on deprived people rather than on, say, economic decline or social inequality. Therefore, it is argued, area policies are ameliorative and deal with the symptoms rather than the causes of urban decay.[13]

Such arguments have some force. Housing stress and decay are inextricably linked to the economic base of the inner cities. But housing decay is more concentrated than most other measures of social deprivation such as poverty or unemployment. And areas do become blighted which accelerates decline but equally they can improve. The density of older housing in urban areas also indicates a need to concentrate renewal resources in pockets of varying size. Systematic action on an area basis also recognises the link between house condition and 'neighbourhood externalities', which was discussed in *Chapter 2*. Improving the quality of the environment helps to boost confidence and provides a focus for community participation. Concentration of resources, both of staff and money, promises to be more efficient and effective than diluting them over a wider area.

But, perhaps the most telling argument in favour of an area dimension to improvement policy is that it generally works. In a number of towns and cities there are areas which have been successfully revitalised in a way which would not have happened without an area approach. Target dwellings and households are more likely to be reached and it is easier for local authorities, in some cases with the active involvement of local building societies, to provide advice and help to residents. Area policies focus attention and overcome inertia through a combination of subsidies, extra resources and special organisational arrangements. Area declaration is an important statement of intent and, given a sufficient commitment of resources, can often encourage residents and lending institutions to invest with confidence in the future. In other aspects of social policy the justification for an area-based approach is more problematic: some policies are best served by universal provision and others are more effectively aimed at specific groups than specific areas. The critique of area-based policies is more properly aimed at all policies which are geared to symptoms rather than causes. Area improvement is a necessary, although not a sufficient condition, for successful housing renewal. But such intervention will be limited in scope if it is not accompanied by a broader package of measures to reduce basic inequalities within society.[14]

Government's Proposed Changes

The Government endorsed the role of area action for improving the housing stock in the Green Paper and stated that

> 'it will continue as a central plank in the Government's policy.'[15]

It proposed to simplify the arrangements for area declaration. It saw little need to have two types of area because the characteristics of HAAs and GIAs have become increasingly similar; and the powers available in each are now virtually identical. Therefore a single type of area — to be known as a Housing Improvement Area (HIA) would be introduced. Legislation will set out the broad criteria which HIAs would have to meet and the Government will retain a power of veto over declaration. But it appears that a HIA would be almost indistinguishable from a HAA in terms of size, housing conditions, time span and the extent of social and environmental problems alongside those of poor housing. Within HIAs, local authorities would have a similar range of powers to those they already have in statutory areas except for the rules governing grant assistance which would be the same there as elsewhere.[16] The 1987 consultation paper did not amplify or alter these proposals other than to change the name of the new single statutory area to Housing Renewal Area (HRA) presumably in recognition of the fact that area action should encompass both renovation and redevelopment.[17]

Enveloping received similar official approval in the Green Paper with the promise of specific legislation to provide a general power for local authorities to institute such schemes. DoE approval of individual schemes would thus not be needed in the future provided they met certain criteria. Envelope schemes would not be limited, as now, to statutory areas but owners would normally be expected, unlike now, to contribute towards their cost.[18]

Assessment

There is a proven need for area improvement policies which provide a statutory framework of more extensive powers and resources than are available elsewhere. This does not require the retention of two separate types of area. The distinction between GIAs and HAAs makes little sense when even in HAAs the predominant tenure is now owner occupation. Local authorities themselves seem to have lost faith in GIAs. Most commentators welcomed the proposal to streamline the system by introducing a single type of area whilst the local authority associations favoured the retention of HAA type powers. But area declaration must bring real benefits to its residents and offer considerable advantages to local authorities.

Although HRAs would be expected to act as the focus for concerted action, the Government does not plan to offer any additional financial incentives (other than to private developers) within areas, but remarkably intends to remove the existing ones. Grants would not be given at preferential rates in HRAs. No mention was made of the role of environmental improvements except to suggest that specific Exchequer contributions for such work might be ended.

The extent to which premium rates of improvement grant are available to houses in statutory areas has been reduced in recent years. Originally only houses in HAAs attracted the maximum rate of grant but in 1980 this was extended to include houses which were unfit, lacking amenities or in substantial disrepair. In 1988, however, priority status was removed from houses which lack amenities or are in substantial disrepair. The aim was to concentrate grant assistance on the most urgent work.[19] This means that priority rates are still available to houses which are unfit or are located in HAAs. This seems sensible and is consistent with SHAC's grant scheme outlined in *Chapter 4*. But the government has not explained why it intends to remove priority status from houses in HRAs.

Future envelope schemes would be jeopardised by the requirement that all owners should contribute to the cost of the work — a proposal which seems to undermine the reason for their success. This was subsequently recognised by the DoE, which now intends to replace enveloping with *'group repair'*.[20] Whatever name is attached to schemes for the external repair of blocks or terraces of houses, their viability would be further prejudiced by the requirement that a high proportion of those included in any scheme be entitled to means-tested grant assistance towards their share of the costs of the work.

What would happen in HRAs is, as in HAAs, largely reliant on the availability of grant assistance and the ability of local authorities to undertake environmental works and special schemes such as enveloping. Taken together, these proposals seem likely to undermine the scope for successful area improvement, and would inevitably slow down progress.

A New Approach to Area Improvement

There is broad agreement that there should be a single type of statutory area with powers similar to those available in HAAs. But an effective programme of area improvement requires a package of measures including;
- a priority rate of grant
- no-cost envelope schemes where appropriate
- an environmental improvement subsidy incentive
- tougher and streamlined compulsory powers (see *chapter 10*)
- the right of residents to participate in the decision-making process and during implementation of the programme

- selective clearance and redevelopment should be an integral part of area policies with adequate compensation for displaced residents
- a five year time limit, with the possibility of an extension subject to DoE approval
- 'after-care' should be a constituent element of areas to sustain improvements once made and to promote good maintenance.

There should be an agreed expenditure programme for a statutory area which should then be accepted as committed expenditure by the DoE.

A number of local authorities have in recent years designated larger areas which, although non-statutory, are based on statutory action and usually include actual or potential GIAs or HAAs. Rochdale's Community Based Action Areas and Stoke's Community Renewal Areas are examples. Their size, often of over 1,000 homes, enables authorities to co-ordinate other aspects of urban renewal, including economic regeneration and town planning. They can help to stimulate confidence among local residents and businesses. Authorities should be encouraged to develop such areas where appropriate.[21]

External repair or envelope schemes should not need to require a contribution from the owners towards the cost. They seem set to have an important future role because they offer the possibility of securing longer term improvement and of generating greater confidence and private investment than more conventional programmes. An unreasonably high quota of households eligible for grant assistance before a scheme could start should not be set. Procedural obstacles should be reduced to a minimum. Broad criteria are needed for envelope schemes, and although a cost assessment is reasonable, it ought to be related to the cost of alternative solutions such as municipalisation.

Summary

Area improvement still has an important role to play in local housing renewal strategies. There is a strong case for an area approach to improvement in areas where poor housing, inadequate facilities and a poor environment are concentrated. This approach helps to raise confidence among residents, to stimulate self-help, private investment and local participation and to deploy staff resources.

Area policies have yet to make a significant contribution on a national scale although many run-down areas have benefited from the intensive activity declaration can bring. Too few HAAs have been declared. It is a cause of concern that area improvement overall has not succeeded in reversing housing decay. There remain many concentrations of bad housing which would benefit to some extent from an area approach.

The present distinction between GIAs and HAAs makes little sense now and the Government's proposal to replace them with a single type of area is a useful administrative reform. But it is difficult to be optimistic about the future of area improvement if this is accompanied by the loss of important financial incentives. SHAC believes that an effective programme for area improvement must include improved financial incentives for individual owners and local authorities, including a priority rate of grant, no-cost envelope schemes and strengthened local authority powers.

References

1. Institution of Environmental Health Officers, *Area Improvement*, 1981, table I
2. ibid
3. DoE Press Notice 384, 21 October 1982,
    Hansard, Written Answer 10 February 1987, Cols. 158-159
4. Mike Gibson, 'From redevelopment to envelopment?: HAAs in Birmingham, *Housing Review* Vol. 28 No. 2, 1979
    Andrew D. Thomas, *Housing and Urban Renewal*, Allen and Unwin, 1986, pp. 125-134
    J. Mc Carthy and M. Buckley, *Birmingham Enveloping Schemes Survey*, Research Bureau Ltd for DoE 1982.
5. DoE, HSC, various issues, HMSO and author's estimate
6. Green Paper, 1985, para. 50
7. EHCS, 1983, table X
8. P. Jones, 'HAAs: the facts', *Housing and Planning Review*, Spring 1980, pp 5-8.
9. DoE, HSC, various issues, HMSO and author's estimate
10. EHCS, 1983, p. 24
11. EHCS, 1983, tables 75 and 76
12. EHCS, 1982, table 25 and EHCS, 1983, p. 23
13. D.V. Donnison, 'Policies for priority areas', *Journal of Social Policy* Vol. 3 No. 2, 1974, pp. 127-135
14. Thomas, op cit, p.112
    Michael Gibson and Michael Langstaff, *An Introduction to Urban Renewal*, Hutchinson, 1982, p. 285
15. Green Paper, 1985, para. 49
16. Green Paper, 1985, paras. 49-52
17. Consultation Paper, 1987, paras. 26-27
18. Green Paper, 1985, paras. 53-60
19. DoE News Release 164, 17 March 1988
20. Consultation Paper, 1987, para. 8
21. DoE, *Good Practice in Area Improvement*, HMSO, 1984

6

Help and Advice for Home Owners

The first part of this chapter looks at the value and variety of the services which exist to help and advise owners with repair and improvement problems, the second outlines recent Government initiatives in support of these services and the third discusses their funding and scope.

Introduction

Home improvement places a considerable burden on owners to identify, undertake and finance the work to their homes. The success of improvement policy in the private sector depends to an overwhelming extent upon voluntary activity by individual owners. But it is evident that a number of factors, in addition to a lack of financial resources or a loss of confidence in an area's future, may act to inhibit activity. Awareness of the importance of regular maintenance and repair may be heightened by a publicity campaign. But many of those households most in need of financial help in carrying out essential repairs or improvements may be unfamiliar with what help is available and its sources or how to go about getting the work commissioned and completed satisfactorily. This suggests that there is a need for individual help and advice in many cases, but particularly among the least well-off. In recognition of this need home improvement agencies have been established in a number of areas. Their objectives are

- to encourage owners to understand the importance of improvement, repair and maintenance

- to establish the best technical solutions to the problems
- to help owners raise finance, through grants or loans
- to organise the appointment of a builder and to supervise the work.

The first agency services were set up by local authorities, and were primarily intended to promote the take-up of grants and to improve the quality of the work undertaken with grant assistance. In recent years, however, a variety of private and voluntary organisations have established agencies often with the aim of targeting their services on groups with special needs such as the elderly. Others focus on areas which can benefit from concentrated help. The emphasis here is usually on offering a complete service from technical assistance (including scheme design and approval, obtaining builder's estimates and supervision of building work) to housing and financial advice (including help with grant applications and obtaining a loan). There are now approaching 200 agencies in England and Wales.

Often, agency services will involve work which is eligible for a grant. Without the individual attention which an agency can provide those who are most in need are less likely to take up grants. Agencies can thus play a positive role in ensuring that help is directed to those people whose homes require repairs or improvement and who need it most.

Variety of Agency Services

The Birmingham House Improvement Service, set up in 1977, is a typical example of a local authority agency whose primary orientation is towards grant work. The service provides a list of approved builders; a standardised contract; a schedule to control building and material costs; supervision of the work; 'decanting' facilities and financial advice. General housing advice and assistance is not ordinarily offered. A fixed fee is charged for these services. Priority is given to grant applicants. Building societies have seconded staff to work alongside the council's in the service's offices to arrange home improvement loans.[1]

The Anchor Housing Trust 'Staying Put' initiative offered elderly owner occupiers an alternative to sheltered housing for which demand far exceeds supply. It was a strikingly simple concept — the provision of advice and help to enable elderly people to remain in their own homes.[2] Eight projects were launched around the country between 1980 and 1985. They have helped 3,500 elderly households with specific advice and support and work to the value of £6 million has been completed. A key feature of the scheme is that each household is offered help in deciding upon the most suitable option for them. If staying put is the best option then project staff provide the necessary technical advice and support, help with applications for grants, loans or other sources of finance, and offer pastoral support. Round about the same time the Ferndale Project in South Wales was laying the foundation for the development of the 'Care and Repair' schemes. They were originally small repair schemes only. There has been a steady convergence between the two since then and although differences remain, 'Staying Put' and 'Care and Repair' have become effectively interchangeable terms for local agency services for the elderly.[3]

The Neighbourhood Home Improvement Agency in Waltham Forest, East London is a partnership of three bodies; the Circle 33 Housing Trust, the Anglia Building Society and the local authority. Running costs are shared between them. Established in 1983 the agency is aimed at low-income home owners from an area of late nineteenth century terraces. There is a strong emphasis on marketing the service and on integrating its work with the local authority's own housing, environmental health and community work initiatives. The building society has earmarked funds for home improvement loans. Staff, who are based in a show house in the area, publicise the scheme through leaflet drops, talks and exhibitions. Advice is provided on obtaining grants and loans. This ranges from help with the forms through to a full specification and architectural service. The survival of this type of agency is, however, jeopardised by the local authority's inability to meet the demand for grants.[4]

A more ambitious scheme is the National Home Improvement Council's 'Neighbourhood Revitalisation Service' (NRS). It aims to tackle the housing renewal problems of large areas of up to 3,000 houses of older housing with the potential for improvement. A national co-ordinator has been appointed to run the scheme and appraise the selection of individual areas. Each project must get the support of the local authority and local financial institutions and prepare an agreed plan for implementation of the programme.

This scheme is a potentially significant advance in helping to channel private finance into home improvement. Four pilot projects were launched in the mid-1980s in the towns of Oldham, Sheffield, Gloucester and Bedford. The scheme is pioneering and is, as yet, unproven in practice. The NRS concept is designed to make the most effective use of limited public resources whilst maximising private investment. But there are signs that some of the early projects have run into difficulty and are not succeeding in attracting sufficient private finance. Of the £1.2 million put into the project in Bedford in its first two and a half years of operation, more than two-thirds came from the public purse in the form of grant-aid. Similar ratios have been experienced in the other projects. To a great extent this may be because the early projects were based in areas which contain high proportions of the most needy people. Only time will tell whether the new projects will attract greater levels of private finance. But already it seems clear that they will be able to achieve little without guaranteed access to sufficient grant funds.[5]

Recent Government Initiatives

Agency services received official approval in the Green Paper and the

Government expressed a desire to legislate to clarify the powers of local authorities and registered housing associations to provide agencies. Nothing was said about central goverment funding although the suggestion was made that local authorities could be allowed to fund services themselves or contribute towards the cost of those run by voluntary or private sector associations. But in either case the bodies concerned would be expected to minimise costs by securing help from the private sector and levying fees where appropriate.[6]

Agency services are the single area covered by the Green Paper which have benefited from subsequent Government initiatives. The Housing and Planning Act 1986 was amended to allow registered housing associations to provide agency services. Later in the same year the Government agreed to meet half the cost of a £6 million initiative to set up fifty new agencies. Half of these were to be developed by the NRS scheme, twenty by 'Care and Repair', and the remainder by the Anchor Housing Trust under its 'Staying Put' programme.[7] A year later 'Care and Repair' received a surprise windfall of extra money from the DoE allowing it to start a further nine new projects.[8]

The White Paper in 1987 made a commitment that elderly people would be helped with minor repairs through the grant system. This proposal has yet to be elaborated but it seems probable that local authorities will be allowed to make small grants for a few minor but essential works to the homes of elderly people. It is not clear how these might interact with the help that is available from the DSS for similar work.[9]

Funding and Scope of Agency Services

Agencies have already proved themselves of great value in helping those owners most in need of sound advice and assistance about home repairs and improvements. The recent *'Inquiry into British Housing'*, chaired by the Duke of Edinburgh, commented:

> 'We see agency services as one of the most interesting and helpful initiatives in urban renewal... We recommend that agency services be encouraged, and that the financial ground-work be examined.'[10]

The recent cash injection by the Government has recognised that one of the main obstacles faced by agencies is the difficulty of obtaining secure funding. This problem has limited the wider spread of agencies. Funding currently comes from a wide variety of sources but much of it cannot be regarded as long-term or secure. The cost of providing a staff intensive service, such as an agency, is prohibitive for many public and private sector institutions. This is one reason why those agencies run by local authorities alone are predominantly grant orientated. Funds from housing associations and other charities cannot be provided indefinitely.

There are no clear sources of finance to cover the cost of providing general or preliminary housing advice or of offering a small repairs service. Charging a fee might be an option for grant related work but it is impossible to consider many of the services offered by agencies as having income generating potential. In addition, of course, most agencies aim to help low-income households who are likely to need to take out a loan to finance, at least some, of the remedial work to their homes. An acceptance of the value of agencies must be matched by public sector finance. Those who have look-ed at the problem agree that:

> '...the only long-term sources of support are local authorities, or cen-tral government, either directly through grants to organisations such as those made under the Housing (Homeless Persons) Act to housing aid centres, or perhaps indirectly through the Housing Corporation'[11]

It is unlikely that local authorities will be able in the current financial climate to offer more support to agencies. The acceptance by the Government of the useful role which they have should be reflected in a firm commitment to provide subsidy to a range of agencies. It has expressed a wish to target assistance to lower income households and agencies offer an important way of getting this help to them. The aim should be to ensure that at least one multi-purpose agency is operating in every large urban district. The Government has implied that in its opinion agencies are still very much in the experimental phase. Any extension of public funding will depend on their performance, which is being closely monitored by DoE and Department of Health sponsored research.

While no legal challenge has been made, there is some doubt as to the powers under which agency services can be operated. It would appear that existing legislation does not permit a local authority to provide a subsidised agency unless it exists simply to guide applicants through the grant system. Authorities may be able to offer more extensive services in statutory improve-ment areas. But the situation is somewhat confused whilst the absence of a specific power to allow a local authority to finance an agency is not satisfac-tory because there may be competing demands for its general funds. The Government's decision to rectify this anomaly is thus welcome.

As the earlier examples show there are a number of ways in which the private sector can contribute to agencies but these are inevitably limited. Given the financial difficulties it seems unlikely that it could play a major role in the provision of agencies without subsidy, except in those cases where substan-tial equity can be realised from the value of property through loans or mor-tgages. But the private sector can and must become more positive. The early signs are that even with an agency service, far too low a ratio of private in-vestment is taking place. But the Government failed to identify or suggest new ways of attracting private investment into home improvement. The removal of tax relief on improvement loans in the 1988 Budget is clearly not a helpful measure.

The role and objectives of agencies are diverse. Some provide a special service for target groups, usually the elderly. Local authority agencies tend to be principally concerned with processing grants and quality control over building work. Both approaches have something to offer to their clientele. But a study of agencies in 1985 expressed concern about the extent to which agencies are polarised towards one approach or the other. Grant orientated schemes, which are almost always the preserve of local authorities, usually operate in isolation from the wider range of housing advice and assistance which is available, particularly for the elderly. On the other hand a household who approached one of the voluntary projects might not receive sufficient assistance with a grant application. The study, while recognising the wide range of needs that had to be met, considered that the prime need was for general advice on the possible options available to householders.

> 'We would favour the wide availability of general advice on renovation problems with specific services such as small repairs for the elderly, full grant agencies and more limited technical packages, available as appropriate to clients' needs'.[12]

This need would probably be best met by a multi-purpose agency which could tailor solutions to a client's requirements more closely. But only a minority of existing agencies are able to offer such a service.

The proposal to introduce a small works grant is welcome. The grant should cover those necessary jobs such as defective guttering, a leaky roof, faulty wiring or redecorating which elderly people in particular are often unable to do for themselves. It should certainly help in those situations where the householder is unwilling or unable to undertake the full range of work which would be required when in receipt of an ordinary grant.

Summary

There is little doubt that agencies can encourage improvement work which might not have taken place otherwise, reduce many of the pitfalls associated with it and make any expenditure more effective. The main unresolved problem remains the funding of agencies. The staff costs associated with providing general and preliminary advice cannot realistically be met by fee income. Other services could be paid for through the grant scheme. Financial institutions can play a greater role than they have up to now but they are limited by the degree of financial risk they can tolerate. Subsidy must come from the government either directly to the service concerned or indirectly via local authorities. Whatever method is chosen in the future and the Government appears to have opted for the former, the involvement of local authorities is crucial. It is they who determine priorities and decide which areas merit attention; and only they can award grants. Without grants many agencies would have little work to occupy them.

Agencies will usually be provided by local authorities or voluntary organisations, and paid for by public subsidy, and work in co-operation with the private sector, chiefly financial institutions and building trades. An exception may be the NRS scheme since it is managed and run by the private sector, but it is likely to continue to rely to a significant extent on the cash injection provided by the Government and its individual projects on that provided by improvement grants. There is a need for a broader type of agency which provides general advice and offers a range of choices. For the future, the part that agencies could play in encouraging regular maintenance and repair should be looked at. Agencies must be able to do more than respond to demand, they must market their services.

References

1. Paper at School for Advanced Urban Studies seminar, R. Taylor, University of Bristol, April 1985
2. Karen Smith, *'I'm Not Complaining': The Housing Conditions of Elderly Private Tenants*, Kensington and Chelsea Staying Put for the Elderly/SHAC, 1986, pp 15-16
3. Nigel Appleton, 'Staying Put' *Housing Review* Vol.37 No. 3, May-June 1988, pp. 102-104
4. BSA, *Helping Owner Occupiers Improve Their Homes*, 1985, pp 9-10
5. Gerry Lowe, 'Co-ordinating the neighbourhood revitalisation scheme,' *Municipal Journal*, 6 April 1984, pp. 494-496
   Neighbourhood Revitalisation, A *Times* Newspaper Special Report, 2 October 1987
6. Green Paper, 1985, paras 21-24
7. DoE Press Release 608, 17 November 1986
8. *Housing Associations Weekly*, 27 November 1987, p.3
9. White Paper, 1987, para. 2.18
   Consultation Paper, 1987, para. 9
10. National Federation of Housing Associations, *Report of the Inquiry into British Housing*, 1985, p.37
11. P. Leather, 'Seeking agency services advice', *Municipal Journal*, 5 April 1985
12. Philip Leather, Alan Murie, Lesley Hayes and Jeff Bishop, School for Advanced Urban Studies, *Review of Home Improvement Agencies*, University of Bristol, DoE, 1985, para. 3.27 and paras. 3.2-3.6

CHAPTER 7

Improvement Incentives

This chapter looks at the effectiveness of the remaining incentives to improvement, in addition to grants, area policies and agency services. It covers a range of incentives, both financial and non-financial, provided by the public and private sectors. It examines a number of proposals to encourage improvement and makes practical recommendations for the future.

Introduction

Home improvement often requires resources that the owner does not possess, hence the need for grants. Market imperfections, such as the influence of 'neighbourhood externalities' mean there is a continued need for special assistance through area-based policies. There are a number of other incentives which might help to encourage improvement activity, especially among owners whose homes are not in a poor state of repair or who cannot get a grant. The most influential are likely to be financial. Lowering the cost of building work; encouraging saving for future repairs and raising the incomes of the poorest households all need to be considered as elements of an effective policy.

There are also a number of non-financial barriers to improvement in the private sector. Many of these can be overcome with the assistance of an agency service but, for example, a lack of knowledge about the need for repair work to one's home is a hurdle which even an expanded network of agencies is unlikely to be able to help the majority of owners surmount. Another deterrent is a lack of confidence in finding a reliable, competent builder.

Financial Incentives

Value Added Tax

When value added tax (VAT) was introduced in 1972, the construction of houses was considered a basic activity which should not be taxed. This remains the case today. But VAT was levied on repair and maintenance work from the outset at the standard rate; now 15 per cent. Improvement work was zero- rated. There is a fine distinction between what is a repair, and so subject to VAT, and what is an improvement, and so zero-rated. This produced endless anomalies, and encouraged evasion and avoidance. Many calls were made to abolish VAT on repair work. In 1984, however, the Chancellor 'solved' the problem by extending VAT to improvement work.

VAT is a disincentive to undertake repair and improvement work because it results in a direct, and perceived, increase in its cost. In addition, it penalises legitimate and responsible builders by playing into the hands of those businesses which are not registered for VAT. Such firms often also produce work of a low standard. It ought to be possible to zero-rate building maintenance, repair and improvement work but there are obstacles to this. It might cost £1 billion a year. The Government has also committed itself to no further significant extension of zero-rating for VAT. Zero-rating repair and improvement work would be beneficial but it cannot be done unless the revenue lost can be found elsewhere and unless the Government is prepared to take a stand against European Community policy. One answer could be to retain VAT on repair and improvement work but to levy it at a rate lower than the standard. Another could be to exempt all work undertaken with the aid of a grant from the tax. Some combination of both could be the optimal solution.

Income and Capital Taxes

The existing framework of tax subsidies to owner occupiers is widely held to be indiscriminate, expensive and inequitable. Their formal incidence is regressive, as they benefit the better-off, and fail to target assistance on households most in need of help. The biggest subsidy is mortage interest tax relief (mitr) which is estimated to cost £4.5 billion this financial year.[1] Capital gains tax exemption is worth another £2.5 billion.[2] Other reliefs or exemptions are estimated at about £3.5 billion annually.[3] The existing tax regime favours house purchase and exchange but offers little stimulus to maintenance or repair. There is a stark contrast between declining real levels of spending on private sector improvements and a buoyant mortgage market, underpinned by subsidy. A recent National Economic Development Office (NEDO) report summed up the impact of housing subsidies as encouraging:

> '...the use of housing for capital gain... At the same time, they subsidise consumption of housing services, favour house exchange, and provide no incentive to repair and maintenance expenditure. The outcome is a growing mortgage debt which finances house exchange at the expense of increasing disrepair.[4]

For owner occupiers income tax relief up to the ceiling of £30,000 was given on the interest on home improvement loans until this year's budget. Its abolition is estimated to yield £200 million in a full tax year.[5] The decision was criticised on the grounds that this saving could have been found elsewhere, that abuse could have been checked by improved vetting procedures, and that it removed one of the few improvement incentives in the tax system. But it is doubtful whether many owner occupiers were significantly influenced one way or another by the availability of tax relief, unless the proposed expenditure was substantial. Moreover the rules excluded tax relief on important items such as repairs to exterior walls or internal plasterwork but included luxury items like constructing swimming pools or landscaping gardens.

The case for the reform of housing tax subsidies has been made by many academics and pressure groups over the years. Proposals have ranged from the elimination of mitr, cutting back or abolishing tax reliefs on housing wealth, to introducing a tax on the imputed rent of owner occupiers. These schemes would all produce increased revenue and a greater degree of tax neutrality between owners and tenants. But few would actually encourage extra spending on maintenance and repair, and some would probably discourage it by drawing new groups into the tax system, such as people who owned their homes outright. If imputed rent income was taxed, it would be possible to offset against tax any spending on maintenance and repair. While this and the other proposals raise wider taxation and social policy issues, it is questionable whether setting repair costs against tax would lead to a better maintained stock. If the aim is to encourage maintenance, the abolition or reduction of VAT might be a more effective and simpler device. Direct tax incentives suffer from another disadvantage: they usually favour higher rate taxpayers and taxpayers in general and offer nothing to those outside the tax system. They are least generous in situations where they are most needed.[6]

Nevertheless revision of the existing tax subsidies in a way which reduces the scale of resources devoted to consumption and exchange would allow the introduction of measures to stimulate the maintenance of the present stock. The high yields which would be achieved could easily fund new allowances and boost grant programmes.

Grants are not a permanent solution to the repair problems faced by poor or marginal owner occupiers. An inability to pay for regular, preventive maintenance will lead to gradual, periodical housing disrepair. An attempt must be made to ensure that the backlog of decay is not simply recycled. Reform of the housing finance system would make it possible to expand and fund extra support for property maintenance. The recent *'Inquiry into British Housing'* recommended the phasing out of mitr and its replacement by a needs related housing allowance which would also replace housing benefit and the housing elements of supplementary benefit (now income support).[7] A comprehensive housing allowance designed to lower the burden of occupancy costs, as well as purchase costs, is one option. Its practicality, and that of other options, ought to be examined further. But the difficulties surrounding any change in the taxation of housing are formidable whilst, in the present political climate, it is unrealistic to expect the willingness to face them.[8]

Savings and Loan Schemes

Public resources are not infinite and many households will not qualify for grant assistance or any new special allowance. There is obviously potential for growth in lending for house renovation, and in schemes which encourage saving for future expenditure.

There have been a number of proposals for schemes in which home owners would save money which could be drawn on only to pay for work to their homes and where a certain level of regular saving would entitle them to borrow the balance of the cost of the work. One, the 'Repair Bond', was suggested by the National Home Improvement Council, under which subscriptions would be collected by the local authority from all owners, who would be entitled to withdraw what they had paid in, plus interest, on presentation of invoices for relevant work to their homes. They would also be entitled to borrow the balance of the cost of the work: the loan being repaid by future savings. The amount of the subscription would be based on the value of the property. The account would pass with the house on sale, so any outstanding debt or credit would be reflected in the sale price.[9]

Such a scheme would amount to compulsory saving although only for new borrowers and owners in receipt of a grant. Otherwise, it would be voluntary. Another objection is that the scheme would make extra demands on local authorities, although these might be limited if the subscription was made an adjunct of the collection of rates or the community charge. This scheme is, in effect, a variant of a tax on the imputed rent income of owner occupiers. An alternative might be for building societies and other lending institutions to require a borrower to subscribe to a maintenance bond, paid as a charge added to mortgage interest payments, and subject to tax relief. Such a scheme could be made a condition of a mortgage, like building insurance. Voluntary subscribers would also need to benefit from tax relief on their contributions, or alternatively the interest on their savings could be tax free.[10]

Another possibility would be to adapt the existing 'Homeloan' scheme which is designed to help first time buyers. Under this scheme, home owners would put money into a special 'Homerepair' account at a building society. Such savings would attract interest in the normal way but withdrawals would only be possible to pay for improvements or repairs. After a time the saver could also have the right to a loan for certain kinds of work. As a further incentive it might be possible to offer a government bonus (as in the Homeloan scheme). The scheme could be entirely voluntary, or it could be made a condition of a mortgage.[11]

Most of the preceding measures are essentially long-term since they concentrate attention on new owners. Their influence on existing borrowers and those without mortgages would be small. Even if special savings schemes were set up, in the majority of cases where large scale works are necessary owners will also need to raise additional money. This is likely to be by obtaining a loan. Loans for home improvement and repair are already made by local authorities (but only to a limited extent), building societies and by other financial institutions. Building society lending in the form of further advances to existing borrowers, the great majority of which are for home improvements, has been increasing in recent years. Further advances' share of new lending rose from around 2 per cent in the early 1970s to over 7 per cent by 1984. Building societies lent £1.75 billion for home improvements in 1984.[12]

It is relatively easy for those with high enough and secure incomes to get a loan to pay for work to their homes. All most lenders require is the ability to repay the loan. In general, a loan is cheaper if the borrower can offer security for the loan. This is why most loans for home improvements are additions to existing mortgages, or sometimes new or second mortgages. Some borrowers take out unsecured or personal loans, usually when they only wish to borrow a relatively small sum. Building societies are now able to offer this kind of loan. DSS help is available for the interest payments on improvement loans, as it is for ordinary mortgage payments, if the person qualifies.

For people outside the normal lending criteria there are schemes which reduce the cost of obtaining a loan. A maturity or interest-only loan is a special type of mortgage available from some lenders, especially the bigger building societies, to elderly people. The actual sum borrowed is repaid from the proceeds when the house is eventually sold. Only the interest is paid during the term of the loan. Maturity loans have often been used to supplement grant assistance. In many cases the interest is met by the DSS so there is no increase in the elderly household's outgoings. Agency services, including the 'Staying Put' and 'Care and Repair' projects, have been central in encouraging the growth of maturity loans.[13]

The concept of maturity loans is often difficult to explain and the limited evidence there is suggests that elderly people, in particular, are generally reluctant to take out loans which will then be a charge on their property. But with the recent decline in the availability of grants, maturity loans have increasingly become the only way for many elderly owners to meet repair or improvement costs, and have often had to meet the full cost of the work rather than a proportion.

In early 1987 a legal tangle threatened this form of lending when building societies were brought within the provisions of the Consumer Credit Act 1974. As a result many societies called a moratorium on maturity loans, fearing that the extra paperwork and administrative costs involved would make this type of lending no longer practicable. In October the Government announced that maturity loans granted via agency schemes would be exempted from the provisions of the Act. This will make life easier for those living in an area covered by an agency service but those who do not — the majority — will still have to cope with a loan regulated by the Act.[14]

For many elderly owners the net value or equity of their home may be the only means by which they might meet the cost of maintenance and repairs throughout old age. Maturity loans are 'once-off' improvement mortgages. Research into the households helped by the 'Staying Put' projects found that maturity loans 'touched only the tip of the iceberg'. Most of the elderly people interviewed would need to find funds in the future to cope with the costs of further improvements, adaptations or regular maintenance and emerging repairs. It was estimated that, assuming average life expectancy, the cost of maintaining a warm, adequately repaired and adapted home might total £11,000 over their remaining years. Some elderly owners have always been able to unlock and make use of the store of wealth tied up in their typically unmortgaged homes by moving to a smaller house. More recently small but growing numbers of elderly owners have been attracted to schemes which enable the equity or capital in their homes to be released as cash or income without having to move. A variety of lenders now offer schemes to help elderly owners who are 'house rich but cash poor', but little attention has so far been paid to their potential.[15]

There are two basic types of scheme. 'Home income plans' in which a loan is obtained against part of the house's value and is used to buy an annuity which provides a monthly income. Part of the income has to be used to pay the loan interest. The maximum loan varies from 60 to 80 per cent of the value of the property with a limit of £30,000 because of the tax relief regulations. At current rates a loan of £30,000 would give a woman aged 75 about £1,500 net extra income annually. 'Home reversion schemes' differ from home income plans as they involve selling the home to the lender either for a one-off cash payment or for an annuity income. The elderly person continues to live in the home on a secure lifetime tenancy at a nominal rent. Reversion schemes offer better annuity income than home income plans as there is no £30,000 limit and no loan interest to pay. A woman of 75 with a house worth £40,000 would receive about £2,300 net extra income annually from a reversion scheme.

These schemes are designed to provide income rather than to make money available for repairs. Maturity loans are a better choice for improvement or repair work. But if an equity release scheme is chosen, part of the income can be used for home maintenance. In both types a lump sum can be given instead of or in addition to income, and that could be used for repairs. The prospect for the future growth of equity release depends on the availability of independent advice to help individuals decide on the various options and most appropriate schemes: the expansion of agency services would appear to offer the best hope here. A review of the interaction between state benefits and any home equity released is also required. The building societies have recognised the importance of this relatively new area of activity by sponsoring research into the housing needs of elderly owner occupiers, concentrating on mechanisms to release equity.[16]

A major problem with home income plans is that so much of the annuity has to be used to pay off the loan interest. Given a low enough ratio of loan to property value, it is possible to allow part or all of the interest, as well as the capital, to accumulate on the mortgage account without threatening the loan's security. The merits of rolling up part or all of the interest are obvious. The main barrier to rolling up the interest is the rule that tax relief cannot be given on the rolled up interest. This means that the interest would mount up at a faster rate and the lending institutions believe this is a major deterrent to this type of scheme. The Government defeated a back-bench attempt to amend the tax rules to allow tax relief on rolled up interest in July 1988.[17]

Equity release schemes are of most value to better-off people living in more expensive homes. If reluctance to borrow for home improvement stems from cost, there may be a case for subsidised loans. Some help towards the cost of a loan is already given. Income tax relief is available on the interest of loans taken out before the budget. Income support, which replaced the supplementary benefit scheme in April, can meet the interest on loans for repairs or improvements. To qualify a claimant must not be in full-time work or have savings over £6,000. But savings over £500 are taken into account and will normally reduce the help available. For those who cannot get a private sector loan, the new Social Fund may help with the cost of minor repairs but any payment is usually recovered by deductions from income support. The new schemes are less generous than supplementary benefit used to be and will undoubtedly deter or prevent many households from undertaking improvements with a loan. It would be possible to give further help either by enabling low-cost private sector loans to be provided or making cheap loans available via local authorities. The AMA has suggested that mandatory loans be offered by local authorities to top up a grant or to help those people outside the normal lending criteria. Although local authorities would be required to tailor mandatory loans to suit individual circumstances, there would be no reduction in cost through additional subsidy, since the AMA's scheme relies on the conventional methods already discussed. This idea would appear to be of little real benefit to those owners already excluded from ordinary sources of loan finance.[18]

A loan has to be seen as an alternative to, or to top up, a grant, since both are designed to fund major improvement or repair works. If 100 per cent grant assistance is available to the least well-off, the case for introducing subsidised loan schemes is weakened. Most owners not eligible for a grant, or not entitled to a 100 per cent grant, should have little difficulty in obtaining a loan, since they are likely to need to borrow a relatively small sum or to have an income sufficient to afford the interest on one. They would also be helped by the expansion of the low-cost loan schemes already provided by the private sector and by the introduction of special savings schemes. Income support already helps those not in full-time work. For those owners who lack the income to afford even a reduced cost loan a 100 per cent grant is more appropriate. The practical problems of running a grant system and a system of subsidised loans in tandem would be considerable. Private sector co-operation is uncertain, particularly during periods of high demand for ordinary mortgages, so a subsidised loan scheme would probably have to be run by the local authorities. For these reasons SHAC cannot see any great benefits in introducing arrangements for subsidised low-cost loans.

Non-Financial Incentives

Publicity and Education

There is a need to convince home owners of the benefits to be gained from ensuring that their homes are kept structurally sound and in a good state of repair and to make widely and readily available the information necessary to prevent, or at least inhibit, any tendency to fail to maintain. The first barrier is that many occupiers simply do not accept that work is needed. The 1981 EHCS found that many owner occupiers were satisfied with what the surveyors judged to be poor conditions. Of those living in properties requiring two or more essential repairs 38 per cent thought the repair state to be better than might be expected or almost perfect. Only 7 per cent saw the repair state as very bad.[19] This evidence indicates that many owners are either unaware of the problem which exists, or underestimate its importance. A number of lessons emerge: the need to promote greater awareness about the importance of repairs, how to identify what work is needed, and the value of carrying out regular maintenance. Part of the message needs to be how small faults can turn into serious problems: a slipped roof tile may lead to rotting roof timbers and eventual structural failure. Agency services, discussed in the previous chapter, will have a crucial role in these tasks. But agencies will not be able to help everyone.

The Green Paper agreed that greater effort was needed to make owners more aware of the need for timely repairs but suggested that it was the job of the building industry to do so.[20]

Reaching existing owners appears to require a programme more suited to a public relations approach, in which advertising and publicity would have prominent roles. The problem of disrepair is so large and the extent of ignorance so great that there is no alternative to the Government taking the lead and itself mounting a publicity campaign. Though, in its initial stages, the impetus must come from central government, once the private sector recognises the benefits it will gain, it should be able to play a greater part. The obvious parallel here is with the campaign to educate the public about energy conservation. The way in which the campaign was organised could take a similar pattern. The 'Save It' campaign began by conveying a general message that energy should be conserved without indicating in detail what steps individuals could take. It then developed to convey more specific messages (e.g. loft insulation) and to indicate where further information could be obtained.

The building industry, materials' suppliers and manufacturers all have an interest in increasing the amount of repair and improvement activity. However, most of their existing promotions are for spe cialist improvement items, like central heating or double glazing. The sort of campaign needed to encourage repairs is rather different from that for improvements because it will need, first of all, to convince people that such repairs are essential.

Building societies and other mortgage lenders are another potentially important channel of publicity. House price inflation has inhibited them from doing more to encourage owners to maintain their houses since it has protected them from potential losses. They should emphasise the importance of regular maintenance and, if necessary, be prepared to insist that such work is carried out. Houses for sale should be subject to more thorough and detailed surveys than is often the case. Periodical re-inspections of mortgaged property should be considered. Advice should be provided to first-time buyers on the financial burdens and responsibilities of home ownership. Lenders could consider employing qualified staff to offer free advice and assistance to their mortgagors.

Another option could be to introduce a scheme similar to that available for legal advice and assistance (commonly known as the 'Green Form' Scheme). Home owners could contact a surveyor participating in the scheme for professional help which would either be free or at reduced cost. The scheme would include property inspections, advice on the work required and the costs involved.[21]

Prospective owners, including young people at school or college, must learn about the financial and other responsibilities which home ownership implies. Educational programmes and courses should be developed which are aimed at future generations of home owners and which reflect the fact that the majority of people are now, and will become, responsible for the upkeep of their homes.[22]

Warranty and Guarantee Schemes

The building industry, particularly that sector specialising in small scale rehabilitation work, has a very poor image. An Office of Fair Trading (OFT) inquiry found that in the period from October 1981 to September 1982 close on 27,000 complaints about repair or improvement work were received by local authority trading standards departments and voluntary consumer agencies.[23] The number of complaints rose to 44,000 in 1984.[24] Such complaints no doubt represented the tip of the iceberg of dissatisfied and disillusioned customers. The list of complaints focused on: failure to keep appointments to assess and price work; inadequate pricing and specification details; failure to start and complete work on time; poor quality workmanship often needing additional work to remedy defects; and lack of an easy procedure to obtain redress when things go wrong other than through legal channels. An associated problem is that *bona fide* firms suffer from unfair competition from 'moonlighters' or 'cowboys', and are tarred by their image. *Bona fide* contractors are estimated to lose work worth about £2 billion a year to the 'black economy'. The Exchequer also loses because 'cowboys' are usually not VAT registered.[25]

There is a need to ensure that legitimate builders perform consistently well and provide adequate redress in cases of failure. There is also a need to distinguish between legitimate builders, and those operating in the 'black economy', who often claim to be cheaper and against whom there is normally little redress, and who are perceived as potentially indifferent performers and are thus to be avoided.[26]

Criticisms of poor performance have in part been met by the introduction of insurance-based warranty schemes by the Building Employers Confederation (BEC) and by the Federation of Master Builders (FMB). The BEC scheme is compulsory and covers disputes which arise during the work as well as defects which occur after completion of the work. It also covers bankruptcy and liquidation during construction or the rectification of defects, if either should occur during the guarantee period. The FMB scheme offers customers a two year guarantee against faults arising from faulty materials or workmanship. But it has a number of deficiencies: first, customers are not protected against a firm which goes into liquidation or becomes bankrupt during the course of a contract; second, it is a voluntary scheme and so far only about 600 of the FMB's 20,000 members have chosen to join.[27]

Only a small fraction of builders in the country are members of warranty schemes. In the absence of a warranty scheme or a recommended code of practice, the customer has little effective redress when things go wrong.

The OFT report suggested that local authorities should exercise stricter control over the standards of work financed by grants or loans either by keeping approved lists of builders or only recommending contractors who subscribe to a warranty scheme. BEC believes that local authorities should only pay grants against invoices (not estimates) from VAT-registered contractors. The safeguards which do exist are essentially intended to protect the consumer. They do not directly improve performance. There is a need for measures to provide the public with an assurance of good standards of work. NEDO recommended introducing a scheme which would offer wholly independent arbitration when complaints were made and be binding on the builder in terms of making good poor or unsatisfactory work. It would aim to have a national standing and reputation equivalent to that of the National House Building Council's scheme for new houses. NEDO also recommended further steps to encourage a greater level of skills and performance in the building industry. In 1987 the DoE set up a working party with representatives from the industry and consumer bodies to look at ways of dealing with the problems caused by 'cowboy' builders. It planned to consider a wide range of aspects including training, warranty schemes, information and taxation. A report is expected shortly.[28]

Summary

More effective incentives to encourage private owners to undertake regular maintenance and repairs are a priority. The existing tax regime is not in accord with this priority. The rate of VAT levied on repair and improvement work should be reduced. The tax incentives and subsidies to owner occupation absorb a significant proportion of revenue yet frustrate the achievement of housing objectives. In particular they encourage consumption and exchange rather than maintenance or repair. They should be reduced to provide the resources for new measures to stimulate renovation and renewal.

New schemes to encourage saving for future expenditure should be considered while there is a considerable potential for the development and promotion of attractive loan packages, especially those targeted towards the elderly. Equity release schemes which boost the incomes of elderly households offer hope for the future. The Government should, where necessary, help and support saving and loan schemes.

New saving and local schemes offer little to the very poorest households. Expanded grant programmes together with more generous social security help appear to be of greater practical assistance to them.

Factors, other than the financial or economic, are responsible for inhibiting adequate maintenance and repair. Ignorance about the importance of property maintenance and a lack of confidence in the building industry are the chief among them. Publicity and education and warranty or guarantee schemes together with agency services can help to overcome these problems.

References

1. Hansard, Written Answer, 12 April 1988, Col. 69
2. HM Treasury, *The Government's Expenditure Plans 1986-87 to 1988-89*, Cmnd. 9702, HMSO, 1986, p.30
3. AMA, *A New Deal for Home Owners and Tenants:A Proposal for a Housing Allowance Scheme*, 1987, pp. 14-15
4. Building Economic Development Committee, *Ways to Better Housing*, National Economic Development Office, 1986, para.5.16
5. Hansard, Written Answer 29 April 1988, Cols 319-321
6. Andrew Walker, *Housing Taxation: Owner Occupation and the Reform of Housing Finance*, CHAS Occasional Paper 9, 1986
   Andrew D.Thomas, *Housing and Urban Renewal*, Allen and Unwin, 1986, pp. 166-170
   Sue Goss and Stewart Lansley, *What Price Housing? A Review of Housing Subsidies and Proposals for Reform*, SHAC, revised edition 1984
7. *Inquiry into British Housing*, National Federation of Housing Associations, 1985
8. Building Economic Development Committee, op cit, Appendix C, paras 11-13
   AMA, *A New Deal...*,op cit
9. National Home Improvement Council, *Improving Our Homes*, 1985, paras 7.00-7.11
10. Institution of Environmental Health Officers, *The Future of the Housing Stock*, 1983.
11. *Homeloan (Special help for first time home buyers)*, Central Office of Information, HMSO, 1982
12. BSA, *A Compendium of Building Society Statistics*, 1985, table B7
13. Rose Wheeler, 'Home equity conversion: development, policy and issues', *Housing Review* Vol.35 No.1, January-February 1986, pp. 5-9
14. *Inside Housing*, Vol.4 No.5, 6 February 1987
    BSA, *Building Society News* Voi.7 No.10, October 1987
15. Rose Wheeler, op cit, p.5
16. David Bookbinder, 'Using the home as capital', *Housing Review* Vol.37 No.3, May-June 1988, pp.104-107
    Rose Wheeler, op cit, p.7
17. BSA, *Response to the Green Paper on Home Improvement*, September 1985
    The Independent, 5 July 1988
18. AMA, *Less Ruin: More Renewal*, 1986, para. 4.12
19. EHCS, 1983, table 15
20. Green Paper, 1985, para. 14
21. National Consumer Council, *Response to the Green Paper on Home Improvement*, September 1985
22. Building Economic Development Committee, op cit, para. 5.21
23. Office of Fair Trading, *Home Improvements*, 1983, para. 3.5
24. Building Economic Development Committee, op.cit, para. 8.8
25. National Home Improvement Council, op cit, para. 11.02
26. Building Economic Development Committee, op cit, para. 8.18
27. Alan Pickstock, 'Foundation stones', *Public Services and Local Government*, September 1987, p.38
28. Office of Fair Trading, op cit, para. 8.2
    Building Employers Confederation, *Response to the Green Paper on Home Improvement*, 1985, para. 13
    Building Economic Development Committee, op cit, paras. 8.23-8.30
    DoE News Release 1, 5 January 1987

CHAPTER 8

Housing Standards

The first part of this chapter looks at the existing statutory housing standards, the second at the Government's plans to revise them, and the third assesses these proposals and suggests an alternative approach.

Introduction

The question of standards is crucial to any consideration of improvement policy. The fact that some houses are termed poor or unsatisfactory presupposes that there is one, or perhaps more than one, standard against which they are being measured. In practice, three standards are currently employed for different purposes.

The first is the **fitness standard**. If a house does not meet this standard and a local authority declares it unfit it has to be improved, demolished or closed. Houses benefiting from an intermediate grant are normally required to meet this standard. The second is that of **reasonable repair**; the condition to be achieved by a property after repairs have been carried out with the aid of a repairs grant. The third is the **target standard** which a house is usually required to meet following an improvement grant.

Fitness Standard

The fitness standard is the basic housing standard. It applies to all types of house or flat irrespective of tenure. The standard dates from 1954, eight years after its introduction was recommended by an official committee which based its proposal on a 1919 Ministry of Health manual. It has been largely unchanged since then, save for a minor amendment in 1969 which added internal arrangement to the list of prescribed matters and deleted the requirement for food storage facilities. It is now defined in the Housing Act 1985. The standard is therefore almost 70 years old and there is little doubt that it needs amending to reflect modern circumstances.[1]

In deciding whether a house is unfit, regard is had to its condition in respect of nine matters. It is statutorily unfit if it is considered so far defective in one or more that is not reasonably suitable for occupation in that condition. The nine matters are:-

- Repair
- Stability
- Freedom from damp
- Internal arrangement
- Natural lighting
- Ventilation
- Water supply
- Drainage and sanitary conveniences
- Facilities for the preparation and cooking of food and for the disposal of waste water.[2]

The fitness standard represents the minimum standard below which human habitation of a house is regarded as unacceptable. Local authorities must take action against a house which does not meet this standard either by securing its improvement (if this can be achieved at reasonable expense), or by removing it from the housing stock. The standard is employed across a wide range of powers. Clearance powers are designed for areas of unfit housing. A higher amount of improvement grant is awarded if a house is unfit. The number of unfit houses is a key determinant of local authority capital spending limits.

The fitness standard is an intervention, not an ideal or even a satisfactory standard. The target standard is probably the nearest there is to a satisfactory standard for an existing house, and it is not an ideal standard. The statutory fitness standard was never intended to reflect social expectations of satisfactory housing but to represent a minimum below which no one would be allowed to live, even by choice. While most people would expect or wish to have central heating nowadays, few owner occupiers would expect it to be enforced upon them.

Compulsory action against an individual's wishes has to be legitimised. Parkinson summarised the problem neatly when he wrote:

> 'The dilemma in a democratic society is that in designing a standard one must, as far as possible, respect the freedom of choice of the individual to live as he pleases and also to protect those who find

themselves living in intolerable conditions. Intervention against personal choice can only be justified on grounds of health and safety or for the greater good of the community.'[3]

Although the fitness standard has been criticised for relying too heavily on health and safety principles, guidance in DoE circulars has interpreted it at a level somewhat above these. In dealing with each of the prescribed matters the circulars offer advice and give examples encompassing 'serious inconvenience', 'accessibility', 'privacy' and 'amenity' as well as health and safety. Local authorities are provided with a range of additional powers to secure the repair or improvement of houses which are not judged statutorily unfit. The purpose of these powers, which are little used, is to prevent housing becoming unfit.[4]

It has often been suggested that the standard is too vague and subjective. It does leave a great deal to the professional judgement of the local authority officer. This has some merit. The standard's flexibility means there is little need for quantitative measurement and allows it to keep roughly in tune with changes in knowledge and technology. But this does mean that over time there are variations in its application. A briefing session for surveyors who were to undertake the 1981 EHCS included a set of slides from 1971 illustrating a house which at the time was considered marginally unfit. The suggestion that this building could be anything but unfit was greeted with incomprehension by everyone in the room.[5]

Whatever the arguments about the merits of a subjective standard, there is a widespread recognition that it does not adequately reflect contemporary opinion about minimum acceptable housing conditions. The omission of any reference to a wc or to personal washing facilities is difficult to justify in the last quarter of the twentieth century. But raising the standard, and thus the number of unfit houses, would have little effect unless extra resources were made available.

Target Standard

Houses or flats improved with the help of improvement grants are usually expected to reach the standard set out below:
- be likely to have a useful life of at least 30 years
- be in reasonable repair
- have all the standard amenities, and meet the following requirements
- be substantially free from damp
- have adequate natural lighting and ventilation in each habitable room
- have adequate and safe provision throughout for artifical lighting and have sufficient electric socket outlets for the safe and proper functioning of domestic appliances

- be provided with adequate drainage facilities
- be in a stable structural condition
- have a satisfactory internal arrangement
- have satisfactory facilities for preparing and cooking food
- be provided with adequate facilities for heating
- have proper provision for the storage of fuel (where necessary) and for the storage of refuse
- have adequate thermal insulation in the roof space.[6]

Government's Proposed Changes

In the Green Paper the Government argued that the existing standard made an accurate assessment of a house's fitness or unfitness too difficult. It proposed a new standard, modelled on that already in use in Scotland, which it claimed would be more objective. But it felt that raising the standard to match rising social expectations was inappropriate because an intervention standard could only be justified where there were health or safety risks. The revised standard would therefore be broadly the same in content as the existing one.[7]

The proposed new standard was widely condemned on the grounds that in several respects it was very much lower than the current standard, and even omitted some items contained in the Scottish version. Disrepair would have to have been both dangerous and structural in order to render a house unfit. Internal arrangement was left out meaning that houses with, for example, steep, winding staircases or narrow, unlit passages would be regarded as fit. A wash-hand basin was not specified although it is included in the list of standard amenities for which a mandatory intermediate grant is available. The Scottish standard's requirement for satisfactory artificial lighting was left out. It was also difficult to see how this standard met the Government's aims. It cannot be a health and safety standard if defects like dangerous electrical wiring, unsatisfactory artificial lighting or inadequate ventilation in the wc or bathroom could not be taken into account. The claim that the new standard was more objective than the old hardly stood up either since it continued, necessarily, to use terms such as 'adequate' and 'satisfactory'. The Government also proposed a simplified version of the target standard.[8]

The 1987 consultation paper contained modified versions of the proposed new standards which are set out below.

Revised fitness standard

A house or flat shall be regarded as fit for human habitation, if, in the opinion of the local authority, it:

- is structurally stable
- is free from serious disrepair
- is free from dampness prejudical to the health of the occupants

- has adequate natural lighting and ventilation
- has an adequate piped supply of wholesome water available
- has satisfactory facilities within it for the preparation of food, including a sink with a satisfactory supply of hot and cold water
- has a suitably located wc for the exclusive use of the occupants
- has a suitably located fixed bath or shower, and wash hand basin, provided with a satisfactory supply of hot and cold water
- has an effective system for the drainage of foul and waste water.

Revised target standard

A house or flat shall be held to meet the target standard if it:

- meets the fitness standard
- is in reasonable repair
- has satisfactory electric wiring and artificial lighting
- has adequate facilities for heating
- has adequate thermal insulation
- is likely to have a useful life of at least thirty years.[9]

Assessment

The modifications made in the consultation paper met many, but not all, of the objections to the Green Paper standard. It is now less reliant on narrowly defined health and safety principles. It will still be used in a similar way as the Scottish standard on which it is based. A house or flat will be unfit if it fails to meet one or more of the list of requirements. It will not permit a cumulative approach unlike the present standard. This allows the effect of several matters, which may be minor in themselves, to be aggregated even though they fall under different headings. The Government argues that the new method will make the standard less subjective. This is doubtful. What is true, however, is that it will prevent a house qualifying for a mandatory grant when only minor items need attention.

The new standard is unlikely to affect the unfitness statistics in any major way although its precise influence is impossible to quantify. To the present 1.1 million unfit dwellings would need to be added those which are fit but lack amenities (the 1981 EHCS estimated 390,000), but from this must be subtracted those unfit because of poor internal arrangement and the unknown number of houses judged unfit owing to disrepair which is not serious.[10]

It is possible that the new standard could in the long term result in more unfit properties. Works done on an unfit house currently produce a property which is better than fit and should remain so from ten to fifteen years. A check list approach merely requires works on the one or more items which make a house unfit. A year later another item on the list could drop into unfitness.

The inclusion for the first time of all the standard amenities is a positive step which reflects modern expectations. All can be supported on health grounds whilst a wc and a sink are already included in the Scottish standard. A kitchen sink, whilst not specified in the current standard, is often held to be an essential component of 'facilities for the preparation and cooking of food...', so a specific reference to this amenity probably does no more than clear up an ambiguity. It is unclear whether a wc located outside the house or flat would satisfy the requirement although this ought not to be critical in deciding if a property is unfit or not. The inclusion of the standard amenities will also simplify the cumbersome, and little used, compulsory improvement procedures.

The removal of internal arrangement, although consistent with the aim of a more objective standard, is a retrograde step. It remains important to home safety. Since the revised standard does not include artificial lighting, a requirement for safe passages and stairways seems doubly important. There is a need to ensure safe movement around those parts of a house not served by natural lighting. Home accident statistics dictate that internal arrangement is retained and extended to include a satisfactory means of access and adequate means of escape in case of fire. Modern patterns of activity in the home, increased longevity and leisure time and the latitude of England and Wales make reliance on natural lighting unrealistic. A requirement for artificial lighting should become part of the new standard. To require mains electricity in isolated rural areas could create problems but an electricity supply from private generators is both practical and reasonable. Space heating is included in the Scottish standard and its lack is certainly a threat to the health of the occupiers. It should be part of the new standard. Facilities for the storage of food should be reinstated. This item was removed in 1969, because of the increasing use of refrigerators, but neither the current nor the revised standard provide for a power supply to a refrigerator.[11]

There have been proposals for radical changes to the standard, most notably from the National Home Improvement Council(NHIC) and the Institution of Environmental Health Officers(IEHO). The NHIC's 'minimum habitable standard' has four sections each sub-divided into mandatory and discretionary categories. A third category would apply when it was impossible to make a house fit at economical cost.[12] The standard is rather complicated — six pages are taken to describe it — and it falls somewhere between an intervention and an ideal standard. Parkinson has also pointed out that it lacks consistency. For example 'ventilation' and 'facilities for the preparation and cooking of food' are discretionary items whereas 'electrical power sockets' are mandatory. Heating standards are specified but because a higher standard is set for the elderly, a house could shift from fit to unfit as the occupants age or change.[13]

The IEHO's single standard is based on the current standard together with the full range of standard amenities, artificial lighting, space heating, loft and sound insulation. This standard was subsequently extended by the AMA to an eighteen item 'Habitation Standard' which includes environmental factors, minimum room sizes, freedom from noxious or hazardous substances and thermal insulation.[14] Both require an overall assessment of a house's condition. Not all the prescribed items would be eligible for a mandatory grant. The IEHO's version makes mandatory grant available to install a bath or drainage system but not, oddly enough, a wc or a piped water supply. It is difficult to justify the inclusion of thermal, and especially, of sound insulation. Noise is a serious social problem, particularly in urban areas, but it is hard to envisage it being solved by physical adaptations of existing houses (even if such were technically and financially practicable). The absence of loft insulation, although unsatisfactory, could hardly be a reason for declaring a house unfit. Both proposals are too ambitious to be considered as candidates for a contemporary intervention standard.

A New Standard of Fitness

There should be a minimum housing standard below which action can be required of and by a local authority. Some measure of public acceptability is required to underpin such a standard. The health and safety of the occupiers and the public must play the major, but not the sole, part in justifying a minimum legal standard. Where a decision is made to intervene against personal choice, it is fair and consistent to offer financial assistance. Thus grant should be mandatory if a house is judged unfit, as proposed in *Chapter 4*. On the other hand, it is in the public interest that owners improve their houses to a higher standard than the minimum and that grant be available in some cases. Two standards, an upper and a lower, are obviously needed. The lower standard should form the basis for compulsory action. The list of prescribed items should be extended to include the standard amenities and some health and safety aspects omitted from the original list. SHAC's proposal for a revised fitness standard is set out below:

A house or flat shall be regarded as meeting the **minimum housing standard** if, in the opinion of the local authority, it:
- is structurally stable
- is free from serious disrepair
- is free from dampness prejudicial to the health of the occupants
- has satisfactory internal arrangement, access and means of escape in case of fire
- has satisfactory provision for natural and artifical lighting and ventilation
- has satisfactory provision for space heating
- has an adequate piped supply of wholesome water available
- has an effective system for the drainage and disposal of foul, waste and surface water
- has a wc suitably located within the dwelling

- has satisfactory facilities for the storage, preparation and cooking of food, including a sink with a satisfactory supply of hot and cold water
- has satisfactory personal washing and bathing facilities with a satisfactory supply of hot and cold water.

Note: Repair includes electrical wiring and sockets.

A house below the minimum standard should either be improved, closed or demolished. Where houses are found unfit they should be dealt with as quickly as possible. In practice, this is an infrequent occurence. In 1983/84 only 24,000 unfit private sector houses were subject to compulsory action — less than 3 per cent of the unfit stock. To meet this problem, the Green Paper proposed that local authorities should be required to carry out regular inspections of their areas to identify the number and location of unfit houses and be placed under an obligation to take action to secure an unfit house's renovation or closure within a period of twelve months.[15] While this approach was generally welcomed, the local authority associations argued that it would be difficult to fulfill such a commitment without extra staffing and resources for grants and to provide alternative accommodation. The timescale might not allow local authorities to deal with owner occupied houses with sufficient sensitivity and discretion. One solution might be to permit short-term remedial works, such as making a house wind and weather proof, while postponing the declaration of unfitness and the carrying out of major renovation works in appropriate cases.[16]

In making a decision as to whether renovation or demolition is more appropriate, local authorities are at present required to assess whether the house can be improved at 'reasonable expense'. In the case of rented property it is generally taken that reasonable expense relates to the tenanted value of the dwelling. If this value is low, renovation frequently seems uneconomic. But once a closing order has been made and the tenants rehoused, the value of the dwelling — now that it is vacant - can rise significantly. The Government proposes to remove the test of reasonable expense and allow local authorities to consider a wider range of options for a single dwelling or an area in deciding between improvement and demolition. This should, it suggested, be backed up with a DoE Code of Guidance setting out the social and economic factors to be taken into account in reaching a decision.[17]

The key factor in considering the options for either a single dwelling or an area should be the renewal strategy of the local authority, and not, as the Green Paper assumes, some narrow cost-benefit analysis. The proposal to drop the test of reasonable expense for individual houses is, however, a welcome one. In reaching a decision on the balance between the clearance or renovation of individual houses and areas, consideration of the external environment, together with an economic appraisal, are both necessary.

A New Target Standard

Where improvements are carried out it is worthwhile encouraging work which not only brings houses up to the minimum housing standard but also puts them into a satisfactory state where they are likely to provide a good standard of accommodation for a number of years. This is especially the case if the work is being carried out with the help of a grant. The target standard is not therefore an ideal standard but a 'cap' on the improvement work which can be grant-aided. Although there has been no great pressure for addition to the existing target standard it is recognised as being deficient in a number of respects, such as the absence of dangerous materials (e.g. asbestos) or security. SHAC's revised standard is set out below.

A house or flat shall meet the **target standard** if it:
- meets the minimum housing (or fitness) standard
- is in reasonable repair
- is substantially free from damp and condensation
- has sufficient electric power sockets
- has adequate provision for the storage of household and personal property, fuel (where necessary) and refuse
- has satisfactory thermal insulation in the roof space
- is secure from unauthorised entry
- is free from dangerous substances
- is likely to have a useful life of at least thirty years

There is also an intermediate standard to be considered. In some cases it will not be possible to improve an unsatisfactory house to the target standard either because it is not economically worthwhile or because the owner is unwilling or unable to pay for all the necessary works. In such cases, it should be a firm requirement that the house is at least in reasonable repair to secure it against early deterioration.

Summary

There should continue to be a basic minimum housing standard below which no one is allowed to live even by choice. A house below this standard should be improved or removed from the stock. But this standard should remain an intervention standard justified on health and safety grounds. The existing fitness standard is out of date and omits some important health and safety aspects. The Government's proposed revised standard needs to be improved in some respects. The new fitness standard should include electrical wiring, internal arrangement and means of escape in case of fire, artificial lighting and space heating. Local authorities should be under a duty to take action against an unfit house within a specified period of time. The new target standard should include freedom from condensation, dangerous substances and security measures.

References

1. Central Housing Advisory Committee, Report of the Standards of Fitness for Habitation Sub-Committee, HMSO, 1946
2. s.604. Housing Act 1985
3. Norman Parkinson, 'Towards a new standard of unfitness', *Housing Review* Vol. 36 No.1, 1987 (Parkinson, 1987).
4. Norman Parkinson, 'Still not a fit standard', *Housing Review* Vol.34 No.6, 1985 (Parkinson, 1985)
5. Alan O'Dell, *Unfitness — is it in the eye of the beholder?*: Paper for the Institution of Environmental Health Officers Congress, September 1985
6. s.468(2) Housing Act 1985 and DoE Circular No.21/80
7. Green Paper, 1985, paras. 61-65
8. Green Paper, 1985, Annex II
   Parkinson, 1985
9. Consultation Paper, 1987, Annex
10. EHCS, 1982, tables 12 and 16
11. Parkinson, 1987
12. National Home Improvement Council, *Improving Our Homes*, 1985, paras 9.00-9.05 and Appendix E
13. Parkinson, 1987
14. Institution of Environmental Health Officers, *Home Improvement — A New Approach (the IEHO's response)*, 1985, p.4.
    AMA, *Less Ruin: More Renewal*, 1986, paras. 3.1-3.7
15. Green Paper, 1985, para.66
16. Association of District Councils, *Home Improvement — A New Approach (the ADC's response)*, 1985
    AMA, *Home Improvement — A New Approach (the AMA's response)*, 1985
17. Green Paper, 1985, paras. 67-68

9

Ethnic Minority
Home Owners

> Black and other ethnic minority people unquestionably experience racial
> disadvantage and discrimination in housing. This chapter looks at the
> link between race and house condition and at the provision of housing
> services to ethnic minority home owners by the private and public sec-
> tors. The final part of the chapter makes recommendations for im-
> provements in these services to help and encourage ethnic minority
> owners to renovate their homes.

Introduction

The housing circumstances of black and other ethnic minority people in Britain are in many ways distinct from, and usually inferior to, those of the white
population. The ethnic minority population is overwhelmingly an urban population. It is concentrated in the older, inner-city areas. Asian and black people
have tenure patterns which are quite distinct from each other and from that
of white people: the same applies to the types of property each ethnic group
occupies, and to the size and quality of the property. These distinctions cannot be ignored if improvement policies in the private sector are to succeed.

 The most recent information on tenure and race is available from the
last national Census. Home ownership is very high among Asian households.
In 1981 almost three-quarters were owner occupiers. At the time the average
for the whole population was 58 per cent. Home ownership was lower among
Afro-Caribbean households at 43 per cent. The average for Asian households

conceals wide variations between different ethnic groups. About 80 per cent of Pakistani households are owner occupiers compared with 50 per cent of Bangladeshi households. In 1981 there were about 350,000 owner occupier households of New Commonwealth or Pakistani origin in England and Wales. Since this figure does not include ethnic minority people born in this country or those born in the rest of the world it can be considered an underestimate. The 1991 Census is likely to ask people to identify their ethnic origin so it will give a more accurate figure.[1]

Tenure and House Condition

There is little reliable or up-to-date national information on the nature and quality of the housing occupied by ethnic minority people. Little research has been carried out and only a few basic facts are known. What sources do exist often have serious limitations. There is only one recent national study of racial disadvantage in Britain including that of housing — that by the Policy Studies Institute (PSI) published in 1984. It was not, however, able to undertake a thorough survey of house condition. But the cumulative impact of what information there is leaves no room to doubt that the housing conditions of ethnic minority owner occupiers are much poorer than those of the white population.

Asian and black owners, in general, occupy property which is less desirable than that occupied by white owners in terms of its age, size and amenities. 36 per cent of Asian and black owners live in houses built before 1919 compared with 29 per cent of white owners. 5 per cent of Asian owners lack exclusive use of a bath, access to hot water or an inside wc compared with 3 per cent of white owners. A third of Asian and 15 per cent of black families have more than one person per room compared with 2 per cent of white home owners.[2]

Up to date national statistics on house condition are not available. The 1981 EHCS did not examine the housing conditions of the ethnic minority population. The previous house condition survey did do so and its results are shown in **Table 15**.

It found that people born outside Europe were twice as likely, and those from the West Indies three times as likely, to occupy unfit property than UK born people. Like the 1981 Census, the 1976 EHCS results are based on birthplace not ethnic group. This makes it impossible to estimate, for example, the true circumstances of Asian households. Most people born in the West Indies are of Afro-Caribbean origin and since there is little reason to think that British born black households' circumstances are very different, the housing conditions of people born in the West Indies are likely to be true for all black households. The 1976 EHCS did not distinguish race and house condition on a tenurial basis.

Table 15 House Condition by Birthplace of Head of Household, 1976, England (% of households)

	Born in UK	Born outside UK	Born outside Europe	Born West Indies
Sound dwellings	82.2	77	68	55
Unsatisfactory dwellings				
non-essential repairs only	2.4	4	3	10
in need of rehabilitation[1]	15.4	19	29	35
unfit	3.6	5	8	13

Note:(1) Lacking basic amenities or needing essential repairs
Source: DoE, 1976 EHCS, 1979, HMSO, table D.2.7.

The 1985 GLHCS provides more recent data by ethnic origin for London. Asian and Afro-Caribbean households in London are more likely to live in unsatisfactory housing than are white UK households. The difference between the two minorities is probably explained by the higher proportion of Asian households who are home owners. A third of Asian owner occupiers in London live in housing which is unsatisfactory. Asian households also have higher average repair costs than any other ethnic group — £4,200 compared to the London average of £3,200.[3]

Table 16 House Condition by Ethnic Origin of Househould, 1985, Greater London (% of households)

Ethnic origin	Unsatisfactory				Satisfactory
	Unfit	Fit but lacking amenities	Fit with amenities in disrepair	Total	
Asian	14	2	14	30	70
White UK	5	2	13	20	80
Afro-Caribbean	6	3	17	25	75
Irish	8	2	19	29	71
Cypriot/Greek/Turkish	2	3	21	26	74
Other/not available	9	2	19	29	71
All households	6	2	14	23	77

Source: GLHCS, 1987, table 3.16

The evidence is that in terms of unfitness and disrepair, people from the ethnic minorities experience much less satisfactory housing conditions than the majority white population.

While the level of owner occupation among all ethnic groups is generally lower in the inner cities than elsewhere, a considerably higher proportion of ethnic minority home owners live in inner city areas than white owners. In inner London, Birmingham and Manchester 44 per cent of Asian households are owner occupiers compared with 29 per cent of white households. A survey of four docklands London boroughs in 1985 found that 49 per cent of Asian households were home owners, 25 per cent of Afro-Caribbean, and 22 per cent of white. Generally speaking, black and Asian owners are concentrated in areas of the oldest, poor quality housing and many improvement areas include a very high proportion of ethnic minority owners.[4]

Access to Loan Finance

Far fewer black and Asian people own their homes outright than white people, as they are generally more recent owners. In the 1970s a number of studies found that ethnic minority owners were more likely than white owners to have financed the purchase of their home by borrowing from insurance or finance companies, or with private loans, at higher rates of interest. The financial burden of repaying the mortgage loan therefore made it more difficult for them to pay for any necessary repairs or improvements to their homes. Building societies have been accused of discriminating against black and Asian people, so that they had to turn to other more expensive sources of finance.[5]

It now appears that black and Asian owners are less dependent on such high cost loans. The proportion with a building society mortgage has increased significantly although it is still lower than that of white owners. Black and Asian owners are also more likely to have a council mortgage than white owners. There is obviously still some difficulty in obtaining a building society mortgage, as the proportion of Asian households borrowing from a bank is considerably higher (12 per cent) than that of white owners (4 per cent).[6]

There may be a number of explanations for the continuing lower use of building society mortgages by ethnic minorities. For example, Asian households may need to buy larger homes than others, which may be in areas not popular with lenders or of poor quality. Black and Asian people have lower average earnings than white people and are less likely to have a home to sell, and may therefore need to buy in areas which lenders feel represent a poor investment. There may also still be examples of discrimination by lenders. An investigation by the Commission for Racial Equality of building society mortgage allocations in Rochdale between 1977 and 1981 discovered lending practices which indirectly discriminated against Asian applicants. It suggested that, while some societies have launched special initiatives for run-down areas which may have helped ethnic minority owners, all societies should examine their policies and practices to ensure that equal opportunity is achieved.[7]

One of the major reasons for not undertaking repairs or improvements is a lack of funds to pay for the work. The PSI survey found that on average white men earn substantially more than either Asian or Afro-Caribbean men — about 17 per cent more. The London docklands survey of 1985 found that two-thirds of Asian home owners earned less than £200 per week compared with 57 per cent of all owners. A higher proportion of ethnic minority owners also lacked substantial savings. With home loans being a greater financial burden on ethnic minority owners, and with fewer resources than white owners, it is clearly more important that grants are targeted to them.[8]

Access to Grant Assistance

While many local authorities now monitor the ethnic origin of applicants for, and allocations of, council housing, very few monitor grant applications or recipients. The 1983 DGE did not look at this issue. It is not therefore possible to make an assessment of how successfully or unsuccessfully grants are targeted nationally towards ethnic minority owners.

The London DGE found that, of those few cases where the race of the recipient was known, 24 per cent of all grants were paid to ethnic minority households (including white ethnic minority households), and 31 per cent of higher value improvement grants. A comparison between the proportion of ethnic groups who occupy unsatisfactory housing with the proportionate distribution of grants in London is set out in the table below.[9]

Table 17 Ethnic Origin of Households Living in Unsatisfactory Dwellings and of Grant Recipients, 1985, Greater London (% of households)

Ethnic Origin	Unsatisfactory Dwellings[1]	Improvement Grant Recipients
Asian	8	16
White UK	70	69
Afro-Caribbean	7	7
Irish	5	2
Cypriot/Greek/Turkish	2	} 6
Others/not available	9	
Total	100	100

Note: (1) All tenures
Source: Author's evaluation based on data from 1985 GLHCS, 1987 and London DGE, 1986

Asian households living in unsatisfactory housing are relatively over-represented among those receiving improvement grants. Since about 90 per cent of improvement grants are paid to owner occupiers, this is again likely to be a reflection of the high level of owner occupation among Asian households. This exercise suggests that in London ethnic minority households are probably not being unfairly excluded from grant assistance but because of the low sample size it does need to be treated with some caution.

Monitoring of grant recipients by the London Borough of Lambeth during the year 1984/85 showed that the proportion of improvement grants given to black owners was very similar to the proportion of owners who were black, while the proportion of repairs grants was slightly lower. This was also reflected in grants given within improvement areas, where the black population was higher than in the borough as a whole. The PSI survey found that a slightly higher proportion of West Indian and Asian owners had received improvement grants than white owners (14 per cent of white, 15 per cent of black and 17 per cent of Asian owners). But because a higher proportion of ethnic minority owners live in homes which are in a significantly worse condition than white owners, it would be expected that they would receive a higher proportion of grants.[10]

One of the reasons the PSI survey found why owners do not apply for a grant is that many are simply unaware of the grant system. It is not surprising that this was true of 15 per cent of Asian owners and 12 per cent of black owners but only of 7 per cent of white owners.[11]

Recommendations

Evidence about the housing conditions of ethnic minority owners, their access to loan finance, and take-up of grant assistance is patchy and often out of date. As a first step, providers of finance and other services should keep and monitor records in order to discover the effects of their policies and practices. Local authorities, many of whom already collect racial data in relation to council housing, should extend this to grants. The Halifax Building Society has just started to monitor mortgage applicants, and other societies and lenders (including local authorities) should do the same.

It is equally important that future national and local house condition surveys seek detailed information on race and house condition, so that the housing needs of ethnic minority households can be assessed and services directed appropriately. The same is true of distribution of grant enquiries.

From the evidence that is available black and Asian owners live in worse quality housing than white owners and therefore positive steps need to be taken to ensure that grants and other forms of support are particularly directed towards them. Providers of loan finance should examine their policies and practices and make sure that no direct or indirect discrimination occurs. Local authorities should increase their efforts at publicising the grants system, focussing attention on the ethnic minority owners in their areas.

Most local authorities focus activity on area improvement. It is therefore crucial that areas with concentrations of black and Asian owners are selected for area declaration. Not only does this direct resources towards these owners but area action allows for a more personal approach, which may be necessary to overcome any particular problems or difficulties which ethnic minority owners may experience. Several authorities have found that by basing area selection on a limited range of physical characteristics (such as the extent of multi-occupation, disrepair, etc) areas with a high concentration of ethnic minority owners with specific improvement problems have been overlooked.

Where required, agency services should concentrate assistance on ethnic minority owners to help provide the more intensive approach which is needed. Agencies may be particularly valuable to ethnic minority households, because comprehensive financial counselling can be given tailored to the specific needs of the local population.

Local authorities should make every effort to employ more ethnic minority staff particularly for posts which have contact with the public. This includes staff in local offices processing grants and translation services where appropriate. The Institution of Environmental Health Officers is concerned to increase the number of ethnic minority environmental health officers. Several local authorities specifically employ ethnic minority officers in their urban renewal sections, including some funded under Section 11 of the Local Government Act 1966 and under trainee schemes for black workers. In addition to employing more staff from the ethnic minority communities, it is essential that staff who deal with the public are trained to deal more sympathetically with all members of the local community and have adequate knowledge and access to back-up services such as translation units and interpreters.

Grant giving practices which discriminate against ethnic minority owners should be stopped. For example, one London authority is very reluctant to allow rear extensions to houses to accommodate a bathroom, but insists that bathrooms be installed in existing bedrooms (or part of bedrooms). For large households this may prevent them from getting a new bathroom, and given the larger size of many Asian households this may be indirectly discriminating.

On the other hand some councils have taken a number of positive steps to use the grant system in a way which helps larger households, for example, by giving grants towards bedroom extensions and loft conversions, or for additional amenities in large single family houses, or by allowing bathrooms to be relocated to provide more bedroom accommodation. Some authorities are also prepared to consider helping exceptionally large families convert two adjacent houses into one. All authorities should consider ways of targeting grants so that they help and encourage ethnic minority owners to improve their homes. As fewer and fewer discretionary grants are available in the current financial climate, the distribution of mandatory grants becomes more important. Authorities should consider the ways in which environmental health action could be used to help the ethnic minority community in their areas.

It has been suggested that many ethnic minority owners might prefer to employ builders from the same community to do improvement work. But some local authorities may be reluctant to approve such firms for grant purposes, because of their small size or lack of experience. Nevertheless authorities should examine whether they are unfairly excluding ethnic minority builders and consider ways of increasing their activity, such as by providing clear information about grant procedures and about appropriate standards.

Where housing associations are making a contribution to housing renewal, authorities should specifically encourage the development of black and other ethnic minority associations and co-operatives. The Housing Corporation is already making some efforts to do this and local authorities should follow this example. Under new guidelines for the use of funds under Section 11 of the Local Government Act 1966 authorities are now able to apply for funding for detached duty posts in voluntary organisations. This opens up wider possibilities for authorities to encourage and support local organisations which aim to bring housing improvements to the local ethnic minority population.

Summary

Black and other ethnic minority owners occupy older homes which provide fewer amenities and are in generally poorer condition than those of white owners. They find it harder to raise loan finance for repairs or improvements. There is no national evidence about the race of grant recipients but some limited London data suggests that ethnic minority home owners are not unfairly excluded from grant assistance. This may not be true nationally. In so far as a low income deters people from undertaking work with a grant, the proposals outlined in *Chapter 4* should concentrate help. But both private and public sectors can do more. Financial institutions should examine their lending policies, and local authorities should do the same with their housing renewal policies and programmes to eliminate discrimination. Where necessary, authorities should provide services which specifically target grants and other forms of help on local ethnic minority home owners.

References

1. Office of Population Censuses and Surveys, Census 1981: Housing and Households; England and Wales, HMSO, 1983, table 11
2. Colin Brown, *Black and White in Britain: The Third Policy Studies Institute Survey,* 1984, table 30
3. GLHCS, 1987, tables 3.1 and 3.17

4. Brown, op cit, table 32
   London Research Centre, The Docklands Housing Needs Survey 1985: Technical Volume, Reviews and Studies Series No. 32
5. V. Karn et al, 'Low income home ownership in the inner city', in *Low Cost Home Ownership: An Evaluation of Housing Policy Under the Conservatives*, P. Booth and T. Crook (eds), Gower, 1986
6. Brown, op cit, table 50
7. Commission for Racial Equality, *Race and Mortgage Lending*, 1985
8. Brown, op cit, table 109
   London Research Centre, op cit
9. London DGE, 1986, table 66
10. London Borough of Lambeth, Housing (Private Sector) Sub-Committee, 'Renovation Grants April 1984 - March 1985'
    Brown, op cit, table 51
11. Brown, ibid

10

Private Rented Housing

> The first part of this chapter looks at the private rented sector and some
> of its problems, the second assesses the Government's planned reforms
> and the third puts forward some ideas to improve the quality of rented
> accommodation.

Introduction

Although the sector has been in decline for most of this century, there are
still almost 1.5 million private rented homes in England. Housing associations
provide another 500,000 homes. Together they represent about 10 per cent
of the stock nationally although the sector's size varies between regions. London
has the highest proportion — around 16 per cent.[1] The range of types of
accommodation is diverse from furnished single rooms in large, old houses
to entire houses let unfurnished. Much of it is insecure and represents poor
value for money for many tenants. Its quality is also a cause for concern. It
is often poor in terms of the availability and sharing of amenities and facilities.
It also contains a very high concentration of housing in poor physical condition.

Profile of the Sector

Homes which are rented privately tend to be older, more unfit and in greater
disrepair than those in either of the other two tenures. One in every five
(370,000) is unfit compared with one in every hundred public sector homes.

A third of all unfit houses are rented privately although (in 1981) the sector amounted to one eighth of the stock. Over two-fifths need repairs costing over £2,500. Almost 300,000 lack at least one basic amenity.[2]

Table 18   Unsatisfactory Houses by Tenure, 1981, England (% of dwellings)

	Private Rented	Owner Occupied	Local Authority/ New Town
Unfit	17.7	4.7	1.3
Lacking at least one basic amenity	13.5	3.3	2.8
Needing repairs costing over £2,500[1]	41.9	21.2	12.0
Needing repairs costing over £7,000[1]	16.4	5.2	1.0

Note: (1) 1981 prices
Source: EHCS, 1982, tables E, H, L and 21

On all measures of house condition, the private rented sector provides a very low standard of accommodation. The EHCS results probably understate the true extent of bad conditions because its classification 'private rented' includes houses owned by housing associations. These are likely to be of better quality than those let by other private landlords. Poor conditions in the sector is closely related to its age — almost two-thirds of houses rented privately were built before 1919[3].

The availability of housing amenities remains lowest in the private rented sector.

Table 19   Housing Amenities by Tenure, 1985, Great Britain (% of households)

	Lacking sole use of		with central heating
	bath/ shower	wc inside building	
Owner occupiers	1	1	79
Local authority/new town tenants	1	1	59
Private tenants — unfurnished	10	6	29
— furnished	36	31	42

Source: General Household Survey 1985, HMSO, 1987, table 5.21.

In London the situation is no different. 28 per cent of the capital's unfit homes are rented privately although only 12 per cent of the stock is provided by private landlords (excluding housing associations). Nearly a half are unsatisfactory in terms of disrepair or number of amenities. Average repair costs are three times those of the public sector.[4]

Within the private rented sector the worst living conditions are found in accommodation which is shared by a number of separate households. The term house in multiple occupation (HMO) is used to describe a variety of shared living arrangements including bedsits, shared houses, lodgings, hostels and often bed and breakfast hotels. HMOs are characterised by the fact that some or all of their amenities and facilities are shared by different households. They usually have a very high level of occupancy. Physical conditions are frequently extremely poor and the safety of tenants is often at risk. HMOs are an important part of the rented market and provide quick access, usually furnished, accommodation for single people and other disadvantaged households. There are estimated to be about 290,000 multi-occupied properties in England and Wales providing accommodation for 2.6 million people. Just over 40 per cent are located in London.[5]

In response to a resurgence of concern about conditions in HMOs in the early 1980s, the DoE initiated a physical and social survey of a sample of shared houses.

Table 20 Multi-Occupied House Conditions, 1985, England and Wales (% of dwellings)

Unfit or in disrepair	59%
Needing repairs costing over £10,000	48%
Unsatisfactory means of escape in case of fire	81%
Inadequate number of amenities	61%
Unsatisfactory standards of management	44%

Source: Andrew D. Thomas with Alan Hedges. The 1985 Physical and Social Survey of Houses in Multiple Occupation in England and Wales, DoE, HMSO, 1986, tables 3.2-3.5 and 3.7

Overall 80 per cent of the HMOs in the survey were assessed as unsatisfactory on at least one of three measures — standards of management, occupancy and provision of amenities. More than nine out of every ten tenants shared a wc and nearly as many shared a bath. A third shared a bath with at least six other people. 40 per cent had to share a kitchen; others had no kitchen at all. Average repair costs were £12,430. The authors of the report concluded that there were some exceedingly squalid conditions within HMOs and that their existence was an indictment of national and local government housing policy over many years.[6]

Private tenants fall into a number of quite distinct groups. The elderly who are concentrated in the unfurnished sector where they have lived all their lives, often in the same house. The young, usually without a family, who are often very mobile together with other transient groups who are both usually found in furnished accommodation. The sector also houses a significant proportion of low-income families of all ages who cannot afford owner occupation or gain access to public sector rented housing. Except for some of the young, and some temporary visitors, the majority of households who rent privately have low incomes. The General Household Survey for 1985 showed the median income of unfurnished tenants to be 48 per cent and furnished tenants to be 80 per cent of the median income for all households.[7] Nearly 60 per cent of private tenants in London in 1984 were found to have household incomes of less than £125 per week.[8] People living in HMOs tend to be poor. The mean income of an HMO household was £90 per week in 1985.[9] Ethnic minority people are concentrated in the furnished sector where the highest rents, least security and lowest space standards are found. 14 per cent of HMO tenants had an ethnic origin other than the British Isles.[10]

Expenditure on Repairs and Improvements

The 1981 EHCS estimated that a mere £216 million (about a tenth of this sum came from grants) was spent on improvements or repairs to private rented houses in England that year. It found that two thirds of rented houses had had no major work done on them in the previous five years. The London survey found that 87 per cent had had no significant work carried out on them in the six years up to 1985.[11]

The fact that little voluntary improvement is undertaken by the owners of private rented housing is underlined by grant statistics. Between 1980 and 1985 15 per cent of grants went to private landlords, yet the 1981 EHCS estimated that 27 per cent of houses with grant potential were private rented. About 16,600 private rented homes were renovated with the help of a grant in 1987 at an estimated public expenditure cost of £60 million. But around 750,000 private rented homes are potentially eligible for a grant. The figures for earlier years are given in **Table 21**.[12]

These figures overstate the amount of voluntary work undertaken. Repair and special grants are normally discretionary. But if an owner has been served with a notice by a local authority specifying that certain repairs or improvements must be carried out, the authority must also provide grant assistance at the maximum rate applicable. A very high proportion of repairs and special grants to landlords are mandatory. In 1985, for example, 62 per cent of repairs grants and no less than 86 per cent of special grants to landlords were mandatory.[13]

Only about 2,000 special grants were made in 1985; almost all for fire

Table 21   Renovation Grants paid to Private Landlords and Housing Associations, England (thousands of dwellings)

	Conversion and Improvement	Intermediate and Special	Repairs	Total
1980	9.4	1.6	*	11.0
1981	7.4	2.8	0.6	10.8
1982	8.3	4.6	3.1	16.0
1983	10.9	6.1	9.3	26.3
1984	12.6	7.0	13.2	32.8
1985	9.7	7.4	10.3	27.4
1986	n/a	n/a	n/a	20.6
1987	n/a	n/a	n/a	16.6

Note: * = negligible
Source: Hansard, Written Answer 20 November 1985 Cols.228-230 and 26 November 1986
Cols.260-262
DoE, HCS December Quarter 1987, Part 2 No.32, table 2.17.

escape works. But this was less than 1 per cent of those HMOs judged to have an inadequate means of escape. At this rate of grant approval it would take over a 100 years to deal with all the unsatisfactory HMOs in England and Wales. The average special grant was worth about £4,300 in 1985 and met just over a third of typical repair costs.[14]

Compulsory Powers

Successive governments have sought to tackle poor housing conditions in the private rented sector and the low level of voluntary improvement (despite the inducement of grant assistance) by giving local authorities a wide range of powers to compel renovation work. Tenants themselves also have a number of statutory and common law remedies.

The chief powers are described briefly below:

☐ Unfit Housing — local authorities must require either improvements or demolition or closure.

☐ Fit Housing — local authorities may require repairs to a fit house which is in substantial disrepair or whose condition interferes materially with the personal comfort of the tenant. In the latter case a local authority can only commence action following complaint by the tenant.

☐ Compulsory Improvement — local authorities can insist on the provision of the standard amenities as well as extensive repairs. Outside a statutory improvement area, action may only be taken in limited circumstances against tenanted property.

☐ Houses in Multiple Occupation — local authorities may require additional amenities and facilities and the provision of means of escape from fire. They have a duty to require means of escape in buildings of at least three storeys with a combined floor area exceeding 500 square metres. There are additional powers to limit the number of occupiers, to improve standards of management and, in extreme cases, local authorities can take over management themselves.

Most of the powers available to local authorities are permissive and little used. They allow authorities to secure repairs and improvements in appropriate cases rather than provide absolute individual rights to a reasonable standard of housing.

Statistics for enforcement activity are no more impressive than those for grants. In 1984 just over 600 formal notices were served on the owners of unfit houses by local authorities in London. There are about 40,000 unfit private rented houses in the city.[15] The special powers to deal with the extra problems found in HMOs are also rarely used. In 1983/84, the latest year for which figures are available, a total of 3,853 notices were served in respect of means of escape from fire. The HMO survey estimated that around 216,000 HMOs (74 per cent) could have been served with a means of escape notice. Therefore 18 notices are served for every 1,000 HMOs deemed to require one. This is an extremely low rate of local authority activity.[16]

The number of orders in force also shows a low level of enforcement action.

Table 22 Number of Orders in Force and of HMOs with Potential for an Order, 1984/85, England and Wales

Type of Order	Number of Orders	Number of HMOs with Potential for an Order
Management Order	5,415	127,600
Control Order	51	11,600
Closing Order	6,662	26,100

Source: Institution of Environmental Health Officers, Environmental Health Report, 1985
Andrew D. Thomas with Alan Hedges, The 1985 Physical and Social Survey of Houses in Multiple Occupation in England and Wales, DoE, HMSO, 1986, table 3.5.

Compulsory repair and improvement clearly plays a minor role in the renewal activities of most authorities. The legislation is complex, difficult to enforce and often of uncertain outcome. It is also not comprehensive. The

procedures involved are time-consuming and staff intensive. The cost of en-
forcing notices and orders is yet another deterrent. A local authority can also
take action under other powers, notably under public health law. They are
used in some cases because the procedures are simpler and quicker but they
rarely achieve permanent improvements to a dwelling.

Government's Proposed Changes

The Green and the later White Papers' ideas on the future of grants for private
landlords differ markedly. The Government's intention to legislate to revive
the rented market is probably the explanation, rather than an acceptance of
the criticisms made about the Green Paper proposals.[17]

The present plan is that landlords will remain eligible for grant
assistance but only on a discretionary basis. Only landlords with regulated
tenancies and those who in future offer new-style assured tenancies would
qualify. A landlord would not be subject to a means-test but account would
be taken of their ability to finance the eligible work from rental income. HMO
landlords who are currently only eligible for special grants will in future also
qualify for grant for the full range of work to make an HMO fit. Tenants would
continue to be eligible for grants in certain circumstances. It would appear
that they too will only qualify for discretionary assistance and will also be subject to a means-test.[18]

The Green Paper considered that compulsory powers against private
housing (other than HMOs) were not justified, apart from houses below the
fitness standard or where a nuisance is being caused to neighbouring property
or passers-by. For unfit houses the powers would be streamlined and cover
both improvements and repairs. Landlords who are unable or unwilling to
renovate their property would no longer be able to require the local authority
to purchase it.[19]

The White Paper did not alter or elaborate on the proposals dealing with
compulsory powers. But the minister responsible Mr Waldegrave announced
in March of this year during the committee stage of the new Housing Bill that
the Government now intended to strengthen local authority powers to get repairs
done. It will become a criminal offence to fail to comply with a repairs notice.
Local authorities will be able to do works in default at an earlier stage, if the
landlord fails to comply with a notice. It will be made easier for authorities
to recoup the cost of works in default. Finally, authorities will be able to serve
a notice in all cases without having first to receive a complaint from the tenant. In June the Government also announced that it intended to consult widely about a series of proposals to tighten up powers to deal with HMOs, which
it hoped would be included in the next Housing Bill. A consultation paper on
HMO powers was published in July.[20]

Assessment

Little more than a tentative assessment can be made about the likely impact of the Government's plans on conditions in the private rented sector. The plans appear in some respects to be provisional, and in others much important detail has been left out. It is not clear, for example, whether grants would also be discretionary if a repairs notice was served. Allowing landlords to charge market rents on new lets from early in 1989 will also have an, at this stage unknown, impact on the sector. Decontrol is most unlikely to even stem let alone reverse the shrinking number of rented homes. But a greater proportion of tenants will undoubtedly have to pay market levels of rent than do so now. There is little reason to believe that this extra money will lead to improved housing conditions in rented accommodation. Raising the profitability of private landlords has been attempted several times in the past in an effort to improve conditions but none has succeeded. Many private landlords already make extremely high returns yet still neglect their property.

The Government has nevertheless concluded that allowing greater profits to be made from rented housing provides less justification for state assistance for improvement. Fewer grants will be made to private landlords. This is certain to lead to greater disrepair, despite the promise to toughen some compulsory powers. But at least the Government has now recognised that if less state financial help is going to be available to landlords in the future, it makes very little sense to weaken a local authority's ability to compel repairs and improvements.

SHAC has reservations about making grants to landlords discretionary in all circumstances. An intervention minimum housing standard should be backed up with mandatory financial help. It should not matter in this context whether the work to make a house fit is carried out voluntarily or compulsorily. Many landlords will continue to have regulated tenancies with rents set below a market level. Grant assistance should be available to them. Others will have insufficient resources to afford often extensive work. Grant assistance to landlords should be aligned with rental income as well as with the particular rent regime. The Government's new ideas on compulsory powers do not appear to go far enough. No recognition has been given of the importance of giving tenants themselves effective remedies where, for example, their local authority fails to act or act promptly. The proposals on HMO powers are too limited to deal with the scale of the problem acknowledged by the Government. The proposal to put HMOs on the same basis for grant assistance as other dwellings is however welcome.

A Comprehensive Code for the Private Rented Sector

The respective merits of the alternative strategies of reviving or phasing out the private rented sector are not the subject of this report. It is generally accepted that it meets the needs of a sizeable number of people who are not adequately catered for elsewhere. It will continue to do so for the foreseeable future. Too much time has been spent discussing the ethics of private landlordism and not enough on the immediate needs of tenants. The principal objective of policy should be to devise an effective system to achieve better quality rented accommodation. This requires a clearer formulation of housing standards, the criteria for grant aid and of the procedures and compulsory powers than is proposed by the Government. The reformed fitness standard suggested in *Chapter 8* should provide a better framework for action. Financial assistance should be offered at a level which will enable owners, whether occupiers or landlords, to meet the required standards. The proposals made in *Chapter 4* to improve the grant system should apply, with some changes discussed below, to landlords as well as home owners. Effective legal remedies should be available to local authorities and tenants alike to prevent landlords neglecting their properties.

The inflexibility of the grant system often renders improvement, whether voluntary or compulsory, totally uneconomic. The result is that little or no work is carried out and the property begins to decay, or a local authority has not only to pay for all the repairs itself but also to buy it from the owner. This ties up scarce public resources. Grant assistance can achieve the same result — a better standard of accommodation — at less cost. Any contribution required from a landlord should be limited to a reasonable amount in relation to the condition of the property and the rental income it produces.

A landlord of an unfit house should be eligible for a mandatory grant. The minimum rate of mandatory grant should however be set at a lower percentage. In any other case grants to landlords should be discretionary, but at a similar rate. This would help to discourage those landlords who postpone work so as to get a higher rate of grant. In either case, a landlord with lettings on fair rents should qualify for a higher minimum rate. Extra help should be available in some circumstances to help meet the difference between the total cost of the work and the minimum rate of grant. If the increase in rental income over a ten year period following improvement was sufficient to meet this difference then no extra payment would be made. If rental income was not sufficient additional grant would be paid. An example of how the scheme would work is given on the next page.

The basic aim of this formula is to ensure that a landlord was no worse or better off as a result of carrying out improvement work, except to the extent that the property's value would increase. Public funds would help provide better quality accommodation for tenants, not bigger returns to landlords. It would be a grant condition for a landlord to register the rents of the property whether let on regulated or assured tenancy terms. A rent officer would assess the appropriate levels of rent if they were not registered at the time

Renovation Grant Scheme for Private Landlords

	£	£
Total eligible cost of the works	10,000	
Grant at 50%		5,000
Net cost to landlord	5,000	
Additional rental income over 10 years(1)	4,000	
Extra grant		1,000
Total grant		6,000

Note: (1) Annual rental income is assumed to increase by 4% of the cost of the works.

of grant approval. This would take account of those situations where rents were already above a reasonable fair or market level. It should also be a requirement that the accommodation is let for at least five years and, if not, the grant should be repaid with interest. One difficulty with a scheme which links grant to rental income is that it could put pressure on tenants to agree to improvements they might not want or be able to afford. This should not be a serious obstacle if the property was unfit but a tenant's veto would probably have to be built into the scheme with respect to additional discretionary work.

Powers to compel improvements are a necessary back-up in the rented sector. The main thrust of renewal policy is and should remain one of persuasion. Offering financial help and creating a climate of confidence in an area should encourage a great deal of voluntary activity by private owners — both occupiers and landlords. But legal pressure has sometimes to be used to deal with those landlords who are prepared to neglect their properties and tenants.

The law governing compulsory repair and improvement is cumbersome and confused. The principal cause is the accretion of a series of different legislative regimes which incorporate overlapping and sometimes conflicting criteria. Very little imposes duties on councils to take action, and none on landlords. Remedies for tenants are not effective. Any reform should aim to build a framework which is readily intelligible, has clear and simple procedures, ensures that the necessary work is carried out with the minimum of delay, has effective sanctions for non-compliance and provides adequate safeguards for tenants.

Powers to act against unfit houses should be retained (see *Chapter 8*), but a different procedure should be followed in the case of rented dwellings from that proposed by the Government. A local authority must serve a repairs notice on the landlord of an unfit property if it is capable of improvement at reasonable expense. If the property cannot be renovated at reasonable expense, or the landlord does not wish to undertake the works, the authority should purchase it, compulsorily if necessary, and rehouse the tenants, if required. Tenants of non-resident landlords should have a statutory right to buy at sitting valuation in either situation. A cheap and simple legal procedure should be available to a tenant to make an authority take action if it was negligent or dilatory. It should be an offence to fail to comply with a repairs notice.

Powers to prevent houses slipping into unfitness should not be abolished. Not only would tenants suffer but the eventual cost to the public purse might be greater if it had to meet some of the cost of repairs to an unfit house. Local authorities should be placed under a duty to serve a repairs notice if a house is in substantial disrepair. Prior representation from a tenant should not be required.

HMO powers need, as the Government now recognises, to be strengthened. Its proposals do not go far enough. Local authorities should be placed under a duty to locate and regularly inspect rented housing in their areas, particularly multi-occupied accommodation, and HMO standards should be included within the national minimum housing standard proposed in *Chapter 8*. HMO landlords should be under a duty to ensure the health, safety and welfare of their tenants. The procedures which allow an authority to take over the management of an HMO in extreme cases should be streamlined. HMO tenants should be able to initiate action to improve their housing conditions if a council failed to act.

Summary

The private rented sector has a very high concentration of poor housing. The worst conditions are found in HMOs. Many tenants are poor and vulnerable. Improvement and enforcement activity are both low. Few grants are made to private landlords. Landlords are reluctant to improve because the result is often a decrease in income. The Government's plans are unlikely to lead to an increase in renovation work. A reformed system which links grant to house condition and rental income should encourage greater activity. Compulsory powers should be retained but in an improved form and the procedures streamlined. Tenants should have access to effective remedies.

References

1. HCS 1976-1986, 1987, HMSO, table 9.4
   HCS, December Quarter 1987, Part 2 No 32, HMSO, table 2.22
2. EHCS, 1982, tables E, H, and 21
3. EHCS, 1982, table 21
4. GLHCS, 1987, p.9 and tables 3.4 and 37
5. Andrew D. Thomas with Alan Hedges, *The 1985 Physical and Social Survey of Houses in Multiple Occupation in England and Wales*, DoE, HMSO, 1986, paras 7.3 and 7.26
   Keith Kirby and Leslie Sopp, *Houses in Multiple Occupation in England and Wales: Report of a Postal Survey of Local Authorities*, DoE, HMSO, 1986, table 20
6. Andrew D. Thomas, op.cit, paras. 2.47 and 7.103 and table 4.8
7. General Household Survey 1985, HMSO, 1987, table 5.14

8. Greater London Council, *Private Tenants in London: The GLC Survey 1983-84,* Housing Research and Policy Report No.5, 1986, table 2.11
9. Andrew D. Thomas, op cit, table 4.4
10. ibid, table 4.3
11. EHCS, 1983, tables 34 and 39
    GLHCS, 1987, table 3.43
12. EHCS, 1983, table 58
13. Hansard, Written Answers 12 May 1986 Col.362 and 26 November 1986 Cols. 260-262
14. Hansard, Written Answers, 26 November 1986, Cols.260-262 and 4 December 1986, Cols 748-749
    Keith Kirby, op cit, para. 55
15. Greater London Council, 1984 Abstract of Greater London Statistics, 1985, table 127
    GLHCS, 1987, table 26
16. Keith Kirby, op cit, table 22
    Andrew D. Thomas, op.cit, table 3.5
17. Green Paper, 1985, paras. 43-45
    White Paper. 1987, paras. 3.1-3.18
    Consultation Paper, 1987, para.5
18. White Paper, 1987, para. 2.18
    Consultation Paper, 1987, paras. 14 and 21
19. Green Paper, 1985, paras. 74-75
20. Hansard, Standing Committee G:Housing Bill, Thirty-Sixth Sitting, 10 March 1988, HMSO, Cols. 1584 — 1585
    DoE News Release 320, 9 June 1988
    DoE, Houses in Multiple Occupation:Consultation Document, July 1988

Appendix One

Summary of the main recommendations and proposals made in SHAC's 1981 report *'Good Housekeeping: An Examination of Housing Repair and Improvement Policy'.*

■ Renovation policy should be part of a coherent renewal strategy, which includes new building and clearance, as well as renovation.

■ A code of minimum acceptable standards of housing should be introduced to consolidate existing standards. This would provide the base line for deciding priorities.

■ Existing renovation grants, together with the insulation grant, should be replaced by a unitary renovation grant available at the discretion of the local authority. The grant could cover up to 100% of renovation costs in order to bring the dwelling up to the minimum standards code, but should be related to the means of the applicant to finance the work from their own resources.

■ Local authorities should retain discretionary powers to reclaim part or all of the grant where grant conditions are breached.

■ Local authorities should be actively encouraged to offer agency renovation schemes, using resources within the authority, to undertake improvement schemes for those occupants of bad housing who are not able to take the responsibility for themselves. This should include provision for temporary rehousing for the duration of the work. This would particularly help elderly residents.

■ Local authorities and housing associations have an important role to play in improving housing conditions by the acquisition and improvement of bad housing. This role is particularly valuable in improving conditions in the private rented sector and in helping owner occupiers who can no longer afford to maintain their homes.

■ Zero-rating of repairs and replacement works for VAT would remove some of the disincentive to owners to repair and maintain their property.

■ Building societies should encourage owner occupiers to undertake repairs and maintenance through a repairs and maintenance savings scheme. This should be eligible for some subsidy from central government.

■ Assistance is required by some owner occupiers who cannot afford regular maintenance or repairs, for example, many elderly and single parents. This should include more realistic allowances for repairs in Supplementary Benefit payments, and direct local authority help with the renovation work.

■ Heavy reliance on the private sector to secure improvements in housing conditions does not ensure that those most in need will be helped. This can only be achieved through an active public programme of renovation and new building to replace those houses which are beyond renovation.

Appendix Two

Letter from nineteen housing organisations to the Secretary of State for the Environment

Rt. Hon Patrick Jenkin, MP   24 July 1985
Secretary of State for the Environment
Department of the Environment
2 Marsham Street
London SW1P 3EB

Dear Secretary of State

HOME IMPROVEMENT — A NEW APPROACH

We are writing to you in connection with the above Green Paper and wish to express certain views at this stage, which we believe are fundamental to the re-consideration of home improvement policy. We have been struck by the amount of common ground between the organisations concerned with this issue. We hope you will take due account of this, and whilst we shall all individually be making some detailed observations in due course, they will embody the principles set out in this letter. We are all pleased that the Government is undertaking a review of this important aspect of housing policy, but we wish to ensure that this opportunity is not wasted. We must say at the outset that we do not believe the proposals will succeed in arresting the decline of the housing stock, and we fear that the rate of decline will be accelerated if these proposals are put into effect in their present form.

One of our major concerns is that the Green Paper contains no estimates of future expenditure or activity levels, in respect of improvement assistance, slum clearance, or enveloping, nor are there any indications as to the impact of the proposals, for example, the number of houses below the new fitness standard or the number of households which are likely to be eligible for assistance. We are not only concerned to ensure that adequate progress and a realistic commitment is made, but moreover, we urgently seek some stability for the local authorities administering the scheme, and for the construction industry to gear up and maintain an adequate response.

We share your view that the primary responsibility for the condition of the housing stock lies with the owner, but we have to say that, realistically, we feel it unlikely that private owners will, or can, do more for themselves. It is, of course, true that **some** owners can do more, but there is a growing problem, particularly amongst the elderly and other low income groups, and in run down areas as a whole. It therefore seems that **greater** incentives, more public investment (better targeted) and some intervention are needed if we are to keep pace with the rate of deterioriation and to reduce the backlog of disrepair and unfitness.

We believe that the details of the Distribution of Grant Enquiry (DGE) are consistent with this view, and it does not reveal major abuse of the scheme. Indeed, it is our view that the major problem is not so much that the better-off take advantage, but that those on low incomes **fail** to take advantage. We would like to see the full results of the DGE published however, and some account taken of the tightening up that has had to take place since 1983.

Further, as our proposals, later in this letter, make clear, we feel that there is still a need for incentives to be given irrespective of the financial circumstances of the applicant in order to stimulate investment in areas that are in decline. In other words, there is still a need for targeting to certain properties as well as owners.

Another matter of particular concern is the impact of the proposals upon local authorities' powers to intervene and enforce proper standards of repair and fitness. It would appear that, in future, intervention would not be possible to arrest deterioration until the *'point of no return'* had actually been reached, or when conditions had become so bad that rescue was almost impossible at a reasonable cost.

The particular problems of the private rented sector, and especially houses in multiple occupation, seem to have been overlooked in the Green Paper. We can therefore only conclude that the present deterioraton and decline in this area will continue.

We are very concerned that the net effect of the Green Paper proposals may be to reduce public expenditure, whilst the housing stock continues to deteriorate. We would welcome any evidence you may have to the contrary and would urge that you give a commitment that any resources *'saved'* by the new targeting arrangements will be redirected into other home improvement activity, and that present expenditure levels on home improvement will not be further reduced. We wish to emphasise not only the need to combat the decline in one of the nation's most valuable assets — the housing stock — but also the beneficial effects of housing improvement in social, environmental and health terms, and the fact that valuable jobs can be maintained and secured for the future.

The Government's Proposals

We welcome and share the intention to simplify the grant structure but, at this stage, would only say that we hope that the practical arrangements can meet this objective as we can foresee some problems which need to be resolved.

We also welcome the proposed *'awareness campaign'*, although this could not, or should not, be left to the home improvements industry (it would in any case be seen as self-interest on their part). Everyone will have their part to play but it should be strongly supported by central government.

Further, we are pleased to see the proposals to encourage better builders and higher standards of workmanship, with more control to be exercised by local authorities. The proposals could have gone further, however, and we hope you will consider giving stronger powers to authorities to prevent bad builders doing this sort of work, to insist upon suitable warranties, and to provide more advice and guidance to building firms offering this service.

If the Green Paper is intended to reduce expenditure and target resources more effectively then the proposed switch from grants to loans and the introduction of means testing are not the best that could be devised and will not secure value for money. They will not encourage improvement, but rather will add to bureaucracy and be a deterrent. However, the concept of a mandatory grant aid to the fitness standard is a good one, but unfortunately negated by the restricted eligibility. We are also very concerned that **no** grant aid will be available above the fitness standard, and would prefer a lower level, or tapering, of grant aid.

Equity loans will be generally unattractive, and we anticipate valuation disputes in many cases and a particular problem in low house price areas where the loan will represent an unacceptably high proportion of the house value. They may be an option for some but should not be considered as a *'mainstream'* form of assistance.

We are particularly worried about the lowering of standards, not simply for their own sake — which is important as we are providing for the future — but also because of the effect it will have on intervention and enforcement. The redefinition of fitness seems retrograde in several respects, for example the use of *'dangerous structural disrepair'* and *'dampness so pervasive as to be a threat to health of the occupant'.* We do not feel that this is consistent with the Scottish *'tolerable standard'* (supported by some in earlier submissions) and needs considerable further detailed discussion. The standards proposed also appear somewhat out of date and, for example, there is no mention of thermal insulation.

The proposals in respect of enveloping, particularly the requirement to levy individual contributions, will virtually end the scheme which, considering its overwhelming success to date, is most unfortunate. The omission of boundary walls may seem a small point, but it is a mean measure which hits at the very heart of area success, i.e. confidence building measures which have a very real impact.

The Green Paper recognises that more clearance will be needed, but this is not backed up by a strategy and resources to tackle the problems. Moreover, the proposals are very sketchy and need to be further developed.

The proposed changes in exchequer support are of particular concern to local authorities. However, we all share the view that this could have very damaging effects, with authorities likely to be both unwilling and unable to meet the commitment to the costs of urban renewal. The lack of support for equity sharing loan costs, and the proposal that they will count against capital allocations, will create further problems.

The Way Forward

We do wish to be constructive, and therefore hope you will give consideration to some proposals of our own. However, we have to say that the key to solving the problems of the older housing stock is more investment — by both public and private sectors. Investment should be better concentrated, but this cannot mean simply targeting assistance to individuals below a certain income level. It is essential that:

(i)   more generous assistance is directed to renovating whole areas of run down and declining stock, in the form of a package of direct public investment, more practical advice and assistance, and the creation of incentives for owners and potential owners to revitalise the properties. A system of area declarations which allows a considerable range of assistance is needed. This would vary from low levels where 'pump priming' was needed to get investment flowing again up to very high levels, including 100% grants and other incentive schemes; and

(ii) those on very low incomes, who find even the present scheme unattractive are given more help. This should again include 100% grants and special assistance will also be needed for householders further up the income scale whose housing costs are already high in relation to income; and consideration should also be given to fiscal and other incentive schemes; and

(iii) finally, any scheme must be simple to administer and easy to understand and backed up by adequate advice and guidance. For most people the process of improvement is difficult and traumatic and one which they will not carry out if they face further complex procedures for receiving grants or loans from their local authority.

These crucial problems are very inadequately addressed in the Green Paper.

We also wish to emphasise the variety of local housing conditions, and therefore we must have doubts as to whether the imposition of **any** national scheme will ever succeed unless if allows sufficient flexibility, and gives the authority the necessary discretion to be able to respond in a variety of ways, with different levels of assistance.

We are sorry that this letter is so long, but it does, at least, reflect the depth of unity of purpose we all share. We hope that the Green Paper is radically restructured, taking account of these and other comments. We will help in any way we can to make progress and, of course, would be more than willing to meet with you to discuss the proposals further, as we regard the changes sought as being vital to the safeguarding not only of the housing stock, but indeed to the very health and well being of the nation.

Yours sincerely

Age Concern (England)
Association of London Authorities
AMA
Building Employers Confederation
Building Materials Producers
Housing Centre Trust
House in Multiple Occupation Group (now the Campaign for Bedsit Rights)
Institution of Environmental Health Officers
Institute of Housing
London Boroughs Association
National Federation of Housing Associations
National Home Improvement Council
National Housing and Town Planning Council
Royal Institute of British Architects
Royal Institution of Chartered Surveyors
Royal Town Planning Institute
SHAC
Shelter
Trades Union Congress